Freestyle

Evangelism as Expressing Jesus

K. KALE YU

ELMORETOWNES

Freestyle: Evangelism as Expressing Jesus

Copyright © 2025 by K. Kale Yu

All rights reserved.

No part of this book may be reproduced in any form or
by any electronic means, including information storage
and retrieval mechanisms, without permission in writing from the publisher,
except by a reviewer who may quote passages from the book in a review.

Elmore Townes Publishing

First Edition: March 2025

In referencing biblical passages, the New Revised Standard Version (NRSV)
is used throughout, unless otherwise noted.

ISBN: 979-8-9926540-2-8

Printed in the United States of America

To future freestylers

CONTENTS

Introduction 7

1: What's Wrong with Evangelism? 21
2: Holy Combustions 38
3: Examples of Holy Combustions 59
4: Holy Combustions Happen in the Soil 82
5: Spark Points 102
6: Speak to Spark Points 119
7: Be You in Christ 142
8: Freestyle Can Be Messy 160
9: There Are No Failures 175

Conclusion 191
Acknowledgments 202
Notes 204

Introduction

On the morning of January 12, 2023, I was on a highway driving westward in the direction of the Smoky Mountains of North Carolina. I remember feeling anxious about the follow-up meeting that I was about to moderate. I wasn't worried about running the meeting as much as what would be said. The follow-up meeting had been scheduled three months earlier when we all met at an evangelism conference in the previous fall.

At the conference, attendees were asked to do something they probably didn't expect. I gave them an assignment: put my evangelism model to the test. I asked them to apply it any way they wished to their congregations for the upcoming Advent and Christmas seasons. We would all get together again in January for a follow-up meeting to discuss the results.

"Why am I putting myself through this?" was a question that entered my mind as I was driving. It was a cold morning in January, but I felt my hands sweat. "What if they say that my model isn't that good?" was another discouraging thought. Such criticism was a possibility. I had no idea what they were going to say. Since the evangelism conference, I hadn't been in contact with any of the participants, so I had no idea how well or badly their projects went (or even if they'd done them).

Honestly, I didn't have to give them evangelism homework. It wasn't necessary to take this extra step. More intrusive thoughts entered my mind: "Who gives conference attendees evangelism homework and then has a meeting to check up on them?" As the guest speaker at the conference, I could have finished the conference with no additional responsibilities, but I wanted to know if freestyle works, especially in the local setting with everyday Christians. After all, what is the point of talking about an evangelism model if it doesn't work? Freestyle is supposed to be useful and practical, but what if it isn't? How can I promote something to the church that doesn't help?

What Is Freestyle?

Freestyle evangelism was developed from my academic research in world Christianity and American religious history. After examining unusual outbreaks of Christian conversions and movements in the United States and around the world, I began to realize that the more potent kind of evangelism wasn't a method or strategy. When Christian communities suddenly break out in ways that were not initiated, or even expected, by missionaries, you realize there are other factors at work. Missionaries tended to dismiss and suppress developments from the grassroots that appeared outside of the Christian "norm." They had reasons to be suspicious but their refusal to acknowledge anything that didn't look or feel

Introduction

"Christian" prevented them from seeing exciting responses from native believers that generated powerful creative expressions. The heart of freestyle is capturing people's raw, potent responses to Jesus–a reaction that often leads to genuine outpourings.

However, Christians have preconceived ideas about what makes evangelism in the church work: develop a strategic approach, assign roles for volunteers, map out the execution of the plan, and provide supporting resources. These assumptions are so powerful that they continue to echo in the way we think about evangelism. We continue to return to, even after disappointments and failures, the same kind of approaches for evangelism.

Freestyle offers an alternative view that might be unfamiliar to people because it doesn't have an objective, goal, or a specific destination of what it should look like in the end. However, as I was driving on the highway to the follow-up meeting, I wasn't sure if the open-ended approach to evangelism would catch on. I finally arrived at the church where the meeting was taking place, and after I parked, I stayed in the car for a moment to pray. I took a deep breath and entered the large fellowship hall. I was surprised to see most people had arrived early and were already seated. They arranged the tables in a U-shaped fashion and had my seat at the bottom of the U—where everyone could see me. I felt my heart palpitating as I got my pens and notepads ready.

The plan for the meeting was simple. Although I was moderating the meeting, the participants would do most of the talking. We would go around and have each person share their experiences. To my left, I saw Dr. Pati Graham, a laywoman from Bryson City United Methodist Church. It was hard *not* to notice her. She had a big smile and was brimming with enthusiasm. She was literally sitting on the edge of her seat. She looked like she was ready to burst with excitement. When the meeting started, I turned to her and said, "Pati, you look like you want to share, so let's start with you."

She paused. She calmed herself and slowly panned the room, to ensure she made eye contact with everyone. Her first words—in a firm, excited voice—were: "Unbridled horse!" I was bracing myself for the worst but I didn't expect that kind of reaction. She described how her evangelism project, "Living Nativity," made her feel like an unbridled horse. At that moment, the internal tension within me disappeared. I realized then that if this evangelism model can make her feel like an "unbridled horse," it has a chance. Needless to say, not everyone's evangelism project at the meeting went as well as hers. In fact, some things did not go as planned but there was enough feedback from that meeting to convince me that freestyle is worth writing about.

Freestyle as Self-Discovery in Christ

Freestyle is a book about evangelism but not in the way you might expect. You won't find a step-by-step formula for how to best explain the gospel. It is not a book that will provide evangelism strategies with new insight to reach people for your congregation. If you associate evangelism with a plan, however, it is understandable since much of our thinking around evangelism centers around following a method. If you search the Internet for articles on how to do evangelism, here are a few examples of what we may find:

- "Ultimate Step-by-Step Evangelism Guide"
- "Creating an Effective Evangelism Strategy"
- "10 Steps for Evangelism"
- "15 Methods of Evangelism that Every Christian Should Know"
- "Steps to Developing a Culture of Evangelism in Your Church"
- "Evangelism: Ten Creative Ways for Church Growth"
- "How to Evangelize: 5 Steps"
- "Effective Evangelism: 10 Methods for Success"

If we attend an evangelism seminar or conference, we want to know *how* to do evangelism. To a great extent, evangelism, as people understand it, is about finding a new and creative insight into the practice of evangelism. What programs can we develop and offer that would attract children and families to church? How can we invite people to church without being intrusive? What is the best way to share the gospel? What is trending in mainstream Christian culture today?

Evangelism programs and strategies require training, planning, and execution. Preparation for evangelism involves learning the method and collaborating with others to work in tandem. The process takes time. Workshops, study groups, curriculum training sessions, seminars, committee meetings, and seminary courses are just a few of the ways churches help people prepare for evangelism. After preparation work is completed, an effortful application of those principles by church members and leaders is required.

However, unlike what many of us assume about evangelism, freestyle evangelism does not offer a plan to be adopted and applied. Freestyle can be a creative, spontaneous, and dynamic experience. When the Holy Spirit steers the car, we may be led in unexpected ways. In Acts 16:6–10, Paul and Timothy had plans of traveling to Asia but God alerted them to go in a different direction three times: "forbidden by the Holy Spirit" (v. 6), "the Spirit of Jesus did not allow them" (v. 7), and a vision of "a man of Macedonia" pleading with him" (v. 9). The Holy Spirit will expand our bandwidth of what evangelism could be.

Freestyle is flexible. It can be a one-time gathering. It can be a long series of events or, even, a nationwide movement. Freestyle evangelism is adaptable by design and can quickly shift to a new direction or break apart into multiple components, each going in a different direction.

Self-discovery is not a term you often hear in evangelism but it is a central theme in freestyle evangelism. Freestyle derives from the simple idea that evangelism is the individual's natural, excited response to meeting Jesus. Freestyle evangelism is the expression of their personal journey. They are doing evangelism without thinking they are doing it because they are simply being themselves.

Introduction

An encounter with Jesus sparks "holy combustions"—a term that will be examined more closely in chapters 2 and 3. The encounter arouses within people a self-initiated desire to make Jesus known. From my research, the need to express Jesus is so strong that they have to make Jesus known to the world—but they release Jesus in a way that makes the most sense to them because they don't know how else to do it. They are simply being themselves, whether that means they do it in a very quiet, soft way or in a loud and boisterous manner. They will combust among friends in their subculture, whether on the farm, in the inner city, or in an online community. The jubilation after meeting Jesus is irrepressible and they may act in ways that seem uncharacteristic of them. Holy combustion is the engine that propels freestyle evangelism forward.

If we can briefly describe the mindset of how we think about evangelism, it would be: "make things happen." Freestyle on the other hand is "let things happen," a subtle but markedly different approach to evangelism. From a freestyle perspective, the best kind of evangelism is authentic. In a world where it can be hard to figure out what's real and what's fake, people are hungering for authenticity. The rise of AI, photo imaging tools, manipulated images and sounds, and the constant stream of information make figuring everything out even more challenging. People have fake social media accounts, profiles, and accounts and knowingly disguise their intentions.

Young people especially are suspicious and view religion with skepticism. Trust levels are low and people's fakenessradar is on high alert for deception. However, authentic encounters with Jesus and with one another are one thing that technology cannot provide. Authenticity is the new currency of evangelism. While we may have difficulty explaining authenticity to others, we know it when we see it.

Create Your Own Evangelism

When individuals freestyle, they are authors of their evangelism. They naturally produce an evangelism that best suits them. In a way, freestyle is a laboratory where Christians stretch to see what their faith can do and evangelism is the outward manifestation of an individual figuring out what "Christ in me" means to them. "Christ in me" is a consciousness in an individual that continues to grow and evolve over time. Individuals need room to work through their ongoing understanding of the supremacy of Christ in their lives. "Christ in me" is a new reality for them, and freestyle takes into account how individuals are grappling with the realignment of their priorities. As Paul wrote, "I have been crucified with Christ; and it is no longer I who live, but it is Christ who lives in me" (Galatians 2:20). Freestyle captures this dynamic and enables individuals to express Christ from whatever stage of faith they may be in.

Freestyle could be interpreted as a postmodern approach to evangelism. Postmodernism says "your truth" is different from "my truth"—the implication being that "your truth" is nice and works for you but don't push "your truth" on me because "my truth" is "my truth" and you should respect my

Introduction

identity and boundaries. Freestyle is simply expressing an individual's "my truth" without pushing any other agenda. No arguing or debating. Just be you—the topic of chapter 7, "Be You in Christ." You and Jesus are at the core of freestyle. Freestyle is an individualized, custom-made platform designed by the individual to release Jesus. Freestyle appeals to the postmodern mind by having "my truth" as the epicenter of the individual's evangelistic expression.

Freestyle has a two-prong approach. First, create an environment that invites the Holy Spirit to ignite holy combustions in people. Secondly, enable holy combustions to spread. Empower combusted individuals to carry out their God-inspired prodding to make Jesus known through their gifts, callings, insights, and experiences. As you can imagine, freestyle starts open-ended and entertains a very large field of ideas. Pastors and church leaders are igniters-in-chief who act open-minded about the possibility of the Holy Spirit stirring within people.

Freestylers ignite holy fire and make it grow brighter but, as you can imagine, it can create unanticipated (and, perhaps, unwanted) issues. An untamed fire can start in places where we didn't expect (or don't want to go). The results of combustions don't always look tidy and orderly because evangelism from a freestyle perspective is a dynamic, creative process. The organic evangelistic expression that emerges from people after they encounter Jesus can appear unfamiliar and messy, which is the topic of chapter 8, "Freestyle Can Be Messy."

Because holy combustions take place in the individual, freestyle evangelism draws out a person's individuality. I didn't know it at the time, but the follow-up meeting turned out to be an incubator for ideas. Listening to one another's evangelism projects was instrumental in sparking creativity and more ideas. Chele Mills, who helped organize "Bee Party," an evangelistic project discussed in chapter 3, found the follow-up meeting stimulating. She said, "The discussions, when we went around the table really increased my energy. I started to get new ideas going through my head. Just taking what other people were talking about and the impact they had and thinking about what an impact this [Mills's project] could possibly have. It really gave me a newfound sense of hope."

During the follow-up meeting, we heard about a radical Blue Christmas service inviting local anarchists to participate. Church members didn't know then, but their participation was a transformative moment for the church and their neighborhood as it thawed tensions and increased cooperation. In another church, members were left to organize an ethnic celebration for New Year's Day and the pastors were surprised at how their members took to the task with self-initiative. A pastor allowed a skit about homelessness during Sunday service that sparked unexpected results. The heartwarming skit, which was written and acted by church members, reminded the church of the many service projects they did for their community that stopped abruptly during the COVID lockdowns. The skit reminded church members of its long-standing history in drama and performing arts and reignited people's passion for service ministries. Needless to say, not all evangelism projects in the meeting were successful. However, as we shall see in following chapters, the release is the most important aspect of freestyle evangelism—not the pursuit of a successful outcome.

Discover Your Stroke

The word *freestyle* is borrowed from the sports world. When we hear freestyle, we often think of sports competitions, such as wrestling, cycling, or skiing. When a competition is called freestyle, there are few or no restrictions on how to participate in that particular competition. In other words, competitors are free to use any style or technique that works best for them.

Freestyle swimming is a good example. In the Olympics, there are four strokes in the swimming events: backstroke, breaststroke, butterfly, and freestyle. For the first three events, swimmers must use the prescribed stroke in order to compete. For the freestyle competition, however, swimmers can choose any swimming stroke or style they wish. While all strokes are available to them, you'll notice that just about every swimmer in the freestyle competition uses the front crawl stroke. That is because it is the fastest stroke.

Similarly, freestyle evangelism doesn't prescribe a particular stroke or method. You might be wondering, if there is no method or strategy, how do freestylers do evangelism? After all, Christians have been relying on methods of evangelism because they provide us with a plan of action on how to proceed but, if we don't have a map, we may feel lost and not know what we are expected to do.

In freestyle evangelism, individuals are tasked with creating their own map. They are released—with the guidance of the Holy Spirit, with discernment and approval of church leaders, and with blessing from their church family. Individuals are to find their stroke using their unique personalities, experiences, cultural insights, and backgrounds as the launching point.

In *Freestyle,* you will find people, like Zacchaeus and the Samaritan woman at the well, two unlikely candidates for evangelism, finding themselves while doing evangelism. They don't have a strategy or a particular working plan. They don't even know that they are "doing" evangelism. They are just being themselves. They are creating their own stroke as they discover more about themselves through their encounter with Jesus.

In today's church, however, people are asked to get behind an evangelistic strategy and program. Most of the time, the evangelism plan is not their own, in the sense of being locally generated from the grassroots, but prepared for them. But what if they are the producers of the ideas instead of being receivers? The creators of their own evangelism? Imagine if everyone in the church pews were activated to freestyle and released their latent evangelistic impulses?

Introduction

Jesus, the Holy Spirit, and Your Passions

Jesus ignites fire in people. The Holy Spirit is the oxygen for the fire. And individuals' passion is the fuel in freestyle evangelism. The more passion, the hotter the fire will be. Authentic evangelism is driven by passion and, in *Freestyle*, we will see examples of everyday people, inflamed with a passion for Jesus, breaking through the limits of what they thought was possible. When people are moved to step out in faith, who knows where and how their passion and gifts will take them? Freestyle enables people to trust their "Christ in me" consciousness to propel them forward to a renewed sense of meaning and purpose.

As you can imagine, people's passions vary and their freestyle expressions will look different coming from a painfully shy introvert, an animated social media influencer, a radical countercultural hipster, an inmate who has served decades in prison, a hyped K-pop fan, a Native American living on a reservation, or a boomer in comfortable retirement. People are hardwired through their experiences, conditions, and subcultures. They shape the way they view themselves and how they understand their world. As a result, few freestyle projects will be the same since the starting point is the individual and Jesus.

From the freestyle perspective, ordinary people without preaching skills, charismatic talents, church culture, or seminary education can combust and produce tremendous amounts of evangelistic energy. Freestyle starts with the premise that people transformed by Christ ignite an irrepressible inner desire to make Christ known. This book is about what happens when ordinary people be themselves in Christ and are released to express Christ in their own way. If that sounds unfamiliar or scary, it is because we don't imagine evangelism as a thrilling experience. Instead, we tend to think of evangelism as "a dirty word," something to avoid, a topic that will be examined in the next chapter.

This is a book about catching fire. Throughout the chapters ahead, I'm going to introduce you to evangelism sparked by spontaneous combustion. People can sometimes combust spontaneously, without anyone's aid or assistance. Freestyling might feel like we are going a little bit out of our depth. However, only when we feel that our feet are not quite touching the bottom can we feel like an unbridled horse—unleashed, unfettered, and free. When we step out in faith, just like Dr. Graham did with her project, we are in a place to do something thrilling, and, perhaps, scary.

CHAPTER ONE

What's Wrong with Evangelism?

If I say the word *evangelism* to you, what words come to your mind? I asked this very question at an evangelism conference. As I discovered from listening to their responses, we have specific ideas of what evangelism means, and none are good. This chapter is about giving voice to those frustrations, and the quotes from the audience will be used later to introduce an examination of the deeper issues. When I asked the question at the conference, no one, at first, said anything; there was just an awkward silence with me standing next to the podium. But I wasn't about to give in. I stood there looking at the audience while they stared back at me.

The standoff went on for a little bit until a brave soul in the back yelled, "A dirty word!" When you consider that the conference was full of pastors, church officials, and lay leaders, you can sense from the comment how deeply frustrated Christians feel about evangelism. The word *evangelism* means "good news" in Greek but it hardly inspires the heart of Christians to venture out into the world.

I walked over to my laptop and typed it out. The words "A Dirty Word" flashed across the big screen. The audience sensed that sharing what they thought about evangelism was fine. Then, comments began to pour out and I continued to type their responses onto the screen until a long list was created. As you might have guessed, people expressed a lot of discontent, but what I found surprising was that the responses had a raw emotional undertone. People can describe something that they dislike but this was different. They vividly described evangelism in terms and ways that were very personal.

How did evangelism turn into "a dirty word"? There are no simple, clear-cut answers. Christians have become deeply suspicious of evangelism. Evangelism is now viewed with so much negativity that the word is no longer used (and, perhaps, practiced) in churches. How does evangelism go from a core, missional principle of the church to a forgotten footnote? If churches give up on evangelism—the only agency in church life specifically designed to share the good news with people—how are churches supposed to survive? Let's begin with a quote from the audience to start a discussion on some of the major issues.

"People want no part of it"

Similar to this quote was the comment, "someone else's job," from the audience. Christians have become unresponsive to the call of evangelism. Survey after survey shows that the dislike for evangelism has been simmering for quite some time. However, their disdain for evangelism should not lead us to think that Christians don't recognize the importance of evangelism, which they do, but they are very much conflicted in how evangelism is conceived and practiced.

This tension is reflected in Barna's conclusions in "Reviving Evangelism" (2019).[1] Across all generational groups, the study revealed that practicing Christians uniformly believe in evangelism. A range of 94 to 97 percent agree that "the best thing that could ever happen to someone is for them to know Jesus." Ranging from 95 to 97 percent, Christians believe "being a witness about Jesus" is part of their faith. Equally unsurprising was the sense of responsibility to be a witness of the gospel, as 96 percent agree that "part of their faith means being a witness about Jesus."

That is the positive news. The negative news is that Christians are walking away from evangelism. The same Barna study showed that millennials and Gen Zers believe evangelism is wrong. They scored higher than other generations in evangelistic potential. Researchers at Barna found that millennials (those born from 1981 to 1996) demonstrate high potential for evangelistic engagement. Nearly three-quarters of millennials say they know how to respond when someone asks questions about faith (73%), and that they are gifted at sharing their faith with others (73%). The percentage is higher than previous generational groups: Gen X (66%), baby boomers (59%), and traditionalists (56%).[2] Not only are they gifted in evangelism, millennials express the most commitment to Christianity. They attended church regularly and "agree strongly" that their faith is "very important."[3]

However, despite all their advantages, there is a problem. They don't believe in evangelism. Forty-seven percent of millennials agree that "it is *wrong* [emphasis mine] to share one's personal beliefs with someone of a different faith in hopes that they will one day share the same faith."[4] Gen Z (born in mid-1990s to the early 2000s) were not included in this study but Barna expects that they too "will likely amplify this stance toward evangelism."[5]

Millennials resist the idea of proselytization or inducing conversions. They are more aware of creating discomfort and offense when sharing their faith. "Sharing the gospel today is made harder than at any time in recent memory by an overall cultural resistance to conversations that highlight people's differences."[6] The opposition to evangelism is not strange at all. The sentiment is more common than most of us would like to admit as it is very much in line with what many Christians think about evangelism. Take for example Allison Barron's article titled, "Evangelism: A Dirty Word?"[7] Barron recalls when she was asked about that dreaded "E-word." Her pastor invited her to a twelve-session Bible study on evangelism. She said, "O...kay?" but she really wanted to say, "Thanks, but no thanks." Barron is a believer but, yet, wonders why evangelism leaves "a bad taste in the mouths of so many people—Christians and non-Christians alike?"

The particular memory that comes to Barron's mind when she thinks about evangelism is Bible camp, specifically as a camp counselor watching over kids during the summer weeks. Kids attended festivals and had fun having their faces painted with the five colors of the gospel "when they *had* to sit and listen to get the pretty flowers drawn on their cheeks—but most of them were not really listening."[8] Kids were celebrated when they said the sinner's prayer for seven days but Barron "wondered how they were doing at home after the high of worship music, games and Bible drills wore off." The thought of doing evangelism creates a sense of unease but, Barron says, "that's never what Jesus intended."

Bryan Stone, E. Stanley Jones Professor of Evangelism at Boston School of Theology, urges Christians in his book *Evangelism after Christendom* to reclaim evangelism from being "a dirty word."[9] In an article in *Church Leadership,* Doug Powe, Director of Louisiana InterVarsity Christian Fellowship, says evangelism is a witness of God's love to people but instead has become "a curse word [that] we want nothing to do with."[10] Evangelism should not be seen as "a dirty word," but Powe admits that the word "conjures up unpleasant images of someone yelling at the top of their lungs on a street corner or strangers knocking on the door on a Saturday morning."[11]

Evangelism doesn't have to be, Beau Crosetto says in *Campus Ministry Today,* "the street sign holder, slick TV preacher, or pushy guy."[12] Crosetto, a campus minister and church planter, certainly believes in evangelism and urges Christians to "find your way to share this good news," but, at the same time, understands evangelism carries a stigma that he calls "today's Christian curse word."[13] When he talks to people, he finds that Christians "cringe at the word evangelism." Crosetto wants people to join him "in changing the perception around evangelism and evangelists" but admits we have a lot of work to do. "Christians I talk to are creeped out by it, uncomfortable, and want to run as far away from 'witnessing' as possible."[14]

With such impressions, it's no wonder Christians struggle to find any motivation or optimism about evangelism. During the discussion at the evangelism conference, someone mentioned that churches have dropped using the word evangelism entirely. Instead of evangelism, the committee is called outreach, missions, or NOW (Nurture, Outreach, Witness).

"Adding Butts in the Pews"

In 2024, I guest preached at a church in Mayodan, North Carolina, where I spoke about freestyle evangelism. After the service was over, people from the congregation approached me to ask questions. A woman in particular gave me a puzzled look. She was unsure of what the goal of freestyle was. She asked me a pointed question: "What's the endgame?"

I wasn't sure what she meant, "You mean, freestyle evangelism?" I asked.

She replied, "Yes. What's the endgame of freestyle evangelism?"

For many Christians, evangelism has an endgame—or at least is supposed to have one. She was trying to make sense of freestyle evangelism but had difficulty putting everything together without knowing what it was eventually leading to. She's not alone in thinking about evangelism this way. Without an endgame to evangelism, we wonder, "Why are we doing this? What is the point of this? Where is all of this going?" We then scramble for answers as questions linger in our minds about what we think might be the purpose of the evangelism activity.

Her reaction to freestyle may not be too far from our own. It sounds strange when you hear about freestyle for the first time because there is no endgame. Our conditioned religious impulses lead us to understand evangelism as a means of reaching an endgame, whatever that may be. Why does evangelism have an endgame? An endgame in evangelism gives us a sense of purpose and direction. It puts everyone on the same page. There are no lingering doubts about the "why" question regarding what we are doing. At the same time, an endgame is precisely why many Christians dislike evangelism.

When someone at the evangelism conference said, "Adding butts in the pews," the comment got chuckles and some "amens" and "that's right" from others. Evangelism, viewed as a way to increase membership and attendance, is not, on the face of it, a particularly strange notion. Churches often see evangelism as the primary means to add people to church, which is exactly the problem. Christians have difficulty embracing evangelism that has an agenda, endgame, or ulterior motive attached to it.

Allison Barron, like many Christians, believes evangelism to be an important part of the Christian witness to the world. She believes in the "Great Commission," referring to the passage in Matthew 28:18–20 where Jesus said, "Go therefore and make disciples of all nations, baptizing them in the name of the Father and of the Son and of the Holy Spirit, and teaching them to obey everything that I have commanded you. And remember, I am with you always, to the end of the age."

However, she was taken aback by an incident when people came knocking on her door to tell her "about Jesus."[15] At first, she was excited about the encounter. She shared with them that she too is a believer. They were, Barron says, "not quite believing me when I said I was already a Christian."

She insisted that she knows Jesus but that didn't matter. They continued to talk as if what she said has no bearing. Their agenda was more important. After she thought about her "uncomfortable" experience, Barron reflected that "maybe talking to random strangers about Christ is valuable." Then she added, "But if we do it without really hearing the person we are talking to, what does that achieve?" To Barron, this person's endgame was obvious; it clearly wasn't about her. Barron raises a good point. What is the point of our evangelism if it is self-serving? People have become increasingly distrustful of these kinds of tactics and can quickly detect an ulterior motive.

"Guilt Trips and Manipulation"

This comment, "guilt trips and manipulation," related to many people's experience at the conference. Instead of being seen as inspirational and heartwarming, evangelism causes discomfort that makes Christians fear or turn away. Christians shrink at the pressure to have conversations about their faith with a friend, invite people to attend a church service, or share how to become a Christian. Being a disciple, they are told, means making disciples, whether by sharing a Bible verse or salvation message with friends, neighbors, and coworkers.

Some Christians respond very well to these challenges, but others feel arm-twisted into doing something they are uncomfortable with. However, not doing it may induce feelings of guilt. Ray Comfort is a street preacher who posts videos of himself confidently approaching and engaging people. Even though he is, by definition, an evangelist, Comfort says, "I don't even call myself an evangelist" because evangelism "makes people feel guilty."[16]

When he wanted to offer courses on evangelism, he was told not to use *that* word in its promotion. If he did, "it will be like pitching to cats to come to a hungry pit bull convention. They will avoid it like the plague." Even though Comfort is a big advocate for evangelism, he admits "it's a turnoff for so many Christians." Evangelism has become a "dirty" word "because of its connotations."

Debie Thomas, a minister at St. Mark's Episcopal Church in Palo Alto, California, says, "It's hard to say the word without provoking a nervous laughter. Or a sanctuary full of frowns and flinches. It's progressive Christianity's big, bad *E* word: *evangelism.*"[17] Thomas admits, "We rarely invite [people to church]. We cringe from invitation like cats from bathtubs." She entreats her members to reconsider the importance of evangelism but it's hard especially when they feel evangelism perpetuates a negative stereotype. Thomas says, "We don't want to repeat the horrific sins of colonialist Christianity. We don't want to come across as judgmental or obtrusive."[18]

Unfortunately, the evangelistic vigor that once powered the growth of Christianity in America in the eighteenth and nineteenth centuries has waned considerably in the past century. The raw evangelistic energy that animated and propelled Christianity in the early years has given way to a kind of toxic asset that no one wants to touch. The reasons for the radioactive reaction to evangelism are manifold. Thomas mentions a few: "We don't believe that the gospel is about securing fire insurance from eternal damnation. We don't believe that we hold a monopoly on spiritual meaning, wisdom, and truth. We don't wish to come across as false in our relationships, feigning love and care in order to manipulate people into signing on a doctrinal dotted line."

Guilt trips and manipulation cut both ways. On one hand, Christians feel manipulated into evangelism when told that they are responsible for the souls of others. Manipulation is what they feel when they sense that people are doing things to make others change. They can recall sermons and messages that stressed the personal importance of evangelizing others to save souls. Youth are told to use their social media to influence their network to spread the gospel. On the other hand, they feel guilt from the obligation to evangelize. Church leaders may question the level of their Christian commitment (or even their faith) if they don't take evangelism seriously.

"Powerful Preaching Which Isn't Me"

Christians will tell you that speaking and witnessing to people is the last thing they want to do. When someone said, "powerful preaching, which isn't me," it means the work of evangelism is so different from who they are that they don't consider ever taking part. Another audience member said, "Fear, especially as an introvert." They point to qualities needed for evangelism, such as gifted oratory skills like Billy Graham or assertive, extroverted personalities that are comfortable with engaging (and clashing, when necessary) with people—traits they know they don't possess. They believe in evangelism as a biblical instruction but don't feel that they are the person to do that. Allison Barron, a staff writer for Christ and Pop Culture, said, "I've always thought evangelism meant I had to be charismatic and good at speaking (I'm not—hence why I'm a writer)."[19] Because we narrowly define evangelism, we take a majority of the Christian population out of the evangelism equation.

When Leah Hidde-Gregory was in college, she took a spiritual gifts inventory test that helps people see which spiritual gifts are most evident based on the answers to questions about faith, gifts, and sense of calling. Much to her surprise and confusion, the test said her top gift was evangelism. As a twenty-year-old, it was hard for her to see it. "Not me!" she said. "You might as well have said my number one gift was brain surgery."[20] In her mind, she was not the kind of person she envisioned doing evangelism. An individual gifted with evangelism, in her mind, was someone "who could quote the Roman Road [a collection of verses in Paul's Epistle to the Romans that encapsulate the salvation message] backwards and forwards."

Even as a college student, she was passionate about Jesus and loved nothing more than sharing Jesus with others but that was different from evangelism. She says, "I only wanted to share because I was excited about what God was doing in my life." Evangelism was the furthest thing from what she wanted to do. "I loved to talk about Jesus, but I would never be pushy or coercive about it."

Researchers with the Jesus Film Project wanted to know what's keeping people from evangelism. They surveyed more than 1,600 Christians about the topic of evangelism.[21] What is different about this survey is that it didn't have answers for them, like a multiple-choice questionnaire. They had to think and come up with their answer to questions like, "What prevents people from sharing their faith?" and "What prevents you from talking about spiritual matters with other people?"

They compiled the answers and categorized them into similar themes and the results were published in the "Multigenerational Survey on Evangelism" (2020). "Fear," according to the report, "was far and away the most significant deterrent."[22] Respondents mentioned "fear," "afraid," or "scared," to describe their reluctance to talk about spiritual topics. Fear applies to a wide array of feelings and situations. People shared that they feared losing or harming relationships. They wanted to avoid tensions or confrontations.

Talking to others is particularly troublesome for those who are reserved or quiet. Speaking on the spot and responding quickly with smart answers are not skills they possess. They may not have an amazing conversion story that will thrill listeners. They are comfortable with fewer friends and more engaged in listening to conversations and building relationships rather than giving powerful messages. When they nurture trust in relationships, they are more than willing to open up about their faith and struggles.

"Certain Theology, My Way or the Highway"

Earlier in the chapter, I mentioned Allison Barron's pastor inviting her to join a Bible study on evangelism. She agreed but not without hesitation. What was she afraid of? Barron says, "I trusted this pastor wasn't going to lead me to strangers' doors so I could stammer Bible stories at them."[23]

For many people, evangelism feels like engaging in a combat of some sort. It's "my way or the highway" as someone in the audience said. Evangelism evokes images of being in battle with those who disagree as it can alienate and divide instead of drawing them closer. Many Christians have a hard time blending evangelism into their theological framework. Evangelism evokes a kind of dogmatism and exclusivism that feels awkward and disrespectful to those of different religions or no religious faith at all. They have come to think of this kind of evangelism as excessive and even insensitive and, perhaps, offensive, which may have led someone from the audience to think of evangelism as a "label of fundamentalist Christian."

To another person, evangelism brought up "visions of Jehovah's Witnesses knocking on your door." I wasn't sure what she meant so I asked if she could elaborate. She continued, "You need to have an answer for them. You need to be ahead of them." This approach sees evangelism as a way to "win the argument." A considerable amount of effort is spent to prove something, usually at an intellectual level. While one person may get the upper hand in the argument, it is at the expense of discrediting the other person. Most of us, I think, shy away from this kind of confrontation. Furthermore, many Christians find evangelism particularly disagreeable when they feel evangelism means talking *at* someone, similar to one-sided lecturing. Christians wonder what kind of purpose this would serve or what it achieves? Bryan Stone also alludes to this dilemma when he says, "Evangelism is perceived as something to be feared, as a barrier to mutual respect, careful listening, open sharing, and cooperation."[24]

To the woman who asked me earlier in this chapter what the endgame of freestyle evangelism is, I answered, "No endgame." I explained, "You go into freestyle without any expectation. There is no sense of you 'doing' evangelism. The moment you feel like you are 'doing' evangelism, it's not freestyle evangelism. The purpose of freestyle is the release. Focusing on release allows for the holy combustion to happen."

Freestyle has no expectations, which means the idea of "success" is not a factor. In other words, you are liberated from agendas, ulterior motives, and condemnation. Too often, evangelism is seen as an obligation or "work," a burdensome task hanging over Christians. Freestyle evangelism enables those who encounter Jesus to express Jesus in their own way—or to "be you in Christ."

In freestyle evangelism, we step aside and invite the Holy Spirit to ignite the holy combustion. Unfortunately, we often get in the way of the Holy Spirit by imposing human limitations on how we think and practice evangelism. Freestyle evangelism cannot succeed without the Holy Spirit for the simple fact that the Holy Spirit is the One who ignites holy combustions. In other words, freestylers expect the Holy Spirit to do the heavy lifting.

"Christians Don't Know How to Reclaim Evangelism"

This comment from the audience sums up the feeling of resignation Christians have about evangelism. Perhaps it's because of the exasperation and fatigue that come with repeated discouraging experiences. Evangelism could also make them feel like they are acting outside of their comfort zones. It's probably a combination of these things and more.

In describing the state of evangelism in today's culture, a pastor at the evangelism conference said, "It's bad."

Church leaders are facing a shift in the way people think about volunteering. People are less willing to volunteer the time that their grandparents once did for church activities. The phrase "quiet-quitting" has emerged since the COVID pandemic and reinforces the notion that people would rather focus their attention on the self and on things outside of church. They don't see making church the main thing in their lives. They've stopped engaging and attend for the minimal amount—if even that. While previous generations found meaning and purpose in church participation, younger generations no longer feel that way. For example, in an article in *The Wall Street Journal* that examines Americans' changing church habits, a woman was previously "an anchor" of her church but "not anymore."[25] When she sees her friends and peers, she observes similar trends. Church has faded in importance as their hectic careers and family lives have crowded out church. With all that was happening, Nuehring says, "It was easier to quiet-quit."

Practicing Christians who quiet-quit also observe a disconnect with church, which may partly explain the phenomenon. No matter what they do, they feel things won't change and neither will they make any difference. Everyday Christians see the political infighting, disconnection between clergy and laity, and corruption and become disillusioned with the way the church has lost touch.

What's Wrong with Evangelism?

The current environment has made Christians wary of having anything to do with evangelism. Despite the baggage that comes with evangelism, Debie Thomas wonders why Christians are so reluctant to share the good news. She says, "What, I have to ask myself every time I shy away from evangelism, is so embarrassing and offensive about this kind of liberative news? About the possibility of justice, healing, and wholeness for people starving of hope?"[26]

Is the situation *that* hopeless? Can evangelism be reclaimed? If we consider evangelism a product of human effort, evangelism will certainly be a lost cause. In the following chapter, "Holy Combustions," we will examine how we are not alone in evangelism. The Holy Spirit is essential to freestyle evangelism, and inviting the Holy Spirit is indispensable in igniting holy combustions. Will every freestyle effort result in a holy combustion? Not at all, but as I will explain in chapter 9, "There Are No Failures," the idea of freestyle redefines our understanding of success and failure in evangelism. But, first, let us examine holy combustions more closely and look at how they propel us to evangelistic action.

CHAPTER TWO

Holy Combustions

This idea of holy combustion, it must be said, sounds a little strange. *Freestyle* talks about individuals combusting and spontaneously reacting, but it's unclear to people that evangelism could be planned and organized around them. Evangelism—the way we have understood and been doing it in churches—involves a linear progression from a concept to steps to realize the goal.

For example, if a pastor wanted to start an evangelism or outreach project, the pastor would introduce the idea to the church council or church leadership board. The church council would discuss the merits of the idea and, if green-lighted, the council would discuss the parameters of such a project and an itemized list of expenses would be presented. If approved, a budget is added to the next fiscal calendar. Then, they can begin mobilizing volunteers or a committee to start the project. If they need more help, the church will send out a recruitment notice that says they need volunteers. Once they have enough people, leaders will hold meetings to assign roles and tasks for the project.

Biker Ministry

Consider the biker ministry that a pastor started in his church. Biker ministry was an evangelism concept that allowed church members to engage people outside the neighborhood, a mission priority set forth by the church. The church happened to be on a road that became part of a popular corridor for bikers. As a recreational sport, cycling has seen a boom across the country. The local government encouraged its growth by making cycling more accessible and biker-friendly. Extensive bicycle networks were created and the church's location became part of the wider route network that connected bikers to state parks, historic sites, and small towns.

Bikers like to ride in groups and it wasn't uncommon to see clusters of bikers riding past the church, especially on the weekends. Since the church was on a popular bike route, the pastor saw this as a great opportunity for evangelism. Churches struggle to get visitors, but there was a situation where a steady stream of people passed the church, albeit on bicycles. The fact that most rode through on the weekends meant that the church could become more visible during worship hours. If the churches made more of an effort to reach out to them, they thought, many may join them for worship.

The pastor explained the concept to his church council. A welcome tent was to be erected on church property that would be visible to all bikers passing through. Signs posted on the lawn and tent would advertise free water and snacks, like nuts and granola bars. Volunteers from the church would sit in the tent and pass out the water bottles, fruit, and snacks. In the tent, church brochures explaining basic information, such as church worship times and Sunday school, would be there for anyone to pick up.

The church council approved the biker ministry plan and they discussed the budget, which was significant when you think about the tent and the food and supplies that were needed on a regular basis. A team of volunteers was needed to erect the tent and take it down every weekend. Someone needed to make sure that water bottles and snacks were in steady supply. If not, they would need to go out shopping. After everything was itemized and the budget approved, they began recruiting volunteers to sit in the tent. They made a timesheet of different shifts where people could sit in the tent to hand out the supplies.

Finally, everything was set. They busied themselves with all the tasks related to the birthing of biker ministry. They erected the tent, set up a table in the tent, stocked the table with water bottles and snacks, stacked leaflets about the church, and had a pair of volunteers behind it. Signs were posted on the lawn and church advertising what they were offering: "Free Water." Church volunteers sat in the tent and waited. Most bikers just passed by the church, but some stopped to get water bottles and snacks. They had conversations with the bikers but very few ever made their way into the church pews. The biker ministry continued like this for a while. About a year later, the pastor left for another church. Shortly afterward, the church members dismantled the biker ministry and it was ended.

Why did biker ministry fail? The idea made sense. Biker ministry was carefully thought out as church members debated its merits. They considered what it would require in terms of financial and volunteer commitments. They gained the input of the council and committees to get it where they wanted.

Biker ministry is an example of a top-down evangelism where those in church leadership provide the ideas and impetus for evangelism, an approach opposite to freestyle—a bottom-up approach—that expects laypeople to come up with the ideas and initiative for evangelism. In freestyle, laypeople take ownership of their evangelism. This idea of empowering the laity to take leadership of evangelism, I would admit, may be difficult for many to accept, especially those in leadership. Freestyle doesn't begin with an evangelistic idea or concept from a pastor, church official, expert, book, or denomination; it begins with an individual and Jesus.

Holy combustion is the moment of spiritual ignition; it propels the soul into action. While the first holy combustion is probably the most memorable, a Christian can experience combustions on a regular basis, such as when Paul instructs us, "Rejoice in the Lord always; again I will say, Rejoice" (Philippians 4:4). The act of rejoicing in the Lord is a mini explosion taking place in the heart over and over again.

Why is holy combustion the central theme of freestyle? People experience a holy combustion for the simple reason that the gospel message itself is combustible. It is infused with life-giving truth that stirs the soul into action. As I explain in *Understanding Korean Christianity*, "Crystallized in-between the pages of the Bible are combustible themes, such as deliverance, liberation, and redemption that may trigger responses in ways that are not foreseeable."[27] In addition, Christ lives in the individual after combustion and the "Christ in me" reality demands release since a combustion triggers a dynamic reaction. The urge to express Jesus can be so strong that the desire to make him known to the world is irrepressible.

Mysterious Fire at Sumo Sushi

In the early morning hours of April 5, 2019, between 3 and 4 a.m., the fire alarm sounded at the Sumo Sushi restaurant in Madison, Wisconsin, and alerted the local fire department. Firefighters rushed to the scene, but the sprinkler system was activated, and the fire was put out. Thankfully, no one was in the building when the fire broke out.

What caused the fire at Sumo Sushi to start? According to the National Fire Data Center in Washington, DC, an estimated 5,900 restaurant building fires are recorded by the US fire departments each year and "the leading cause" of all restaurant building fires is cooking equipment at 57 percent.[28] An example is hot cooking oil spilling over onto an open stove flame, igniting a small fire, or a deep fryer near gas ranges catching fire.

As fire officials entered Sumo Sushi, they went through the most plausible causes in their minds. What is interesting about the fire at Sumo Sushi is that none of the usual suspected factors started the fire. After the investigation, officials declared the cause was tempura flakes—yes, tempura flakes, those crunchy morsels that they use to garnish the tops of sushi rolls. People were baffled. You may wonder, "How could tempura flakes start a fire?" Then, something unusual happened. The same exact thing happened at Takara, another sushi restaurant in Madison, Wisconsin, a little more than a month later on May 10, with tempura flakes again as the cause of the restaurant fire.

People discovered that, in the process of making the deep-fried extra crunchy tempura flakes, they need to be cooled off for a long time. They are too hot to eat. Sushi chefs leave the tempura flakes in the kitchen overnight to cool and this is where things can go wrong.

The security camera footage in Sumo's kitchen confirmed the fire officials' findings. It showed tempura flakes in a metal bowl self-combusting.[29] They caught fire on their own—with no help from anyone or anything. Smoke began billowing; the fire grew and spread to other parts of the kitchen. A fire investigator with the Madison Fire Department noted that a unique set of conditions produced the fire. If the tempura flakes had been scattered and laid out flat onto a sheet, the fire probably would not have happened. However, the tempura flakes were piled high in a bowl. The flakes, deep-fried in vegetable or soybean oil, have the ability to self-heat when combined with oxygen. When put together, the self-heating led to spontaneous combustion.

How do self-combusting tempura flakes relate to freestyle evangelism? In a given situation with the proper conditions, people can combust in Christ and, just like these tempura flakes, catch fire seemingly on their own with the critical role of the Holy Spirit as the firestarter. Freestyle evangelism is powered by the natural self-heating release from the combustion. Tempura flakes are probably one of the last things in our minds catching fire and that is exactly the premise of freestyle evangelism. The unusual, overlooked, unexpected, and unlikely are ripe for self-combustion.

The Explosion of Washburn A Mill

There was something very strange and mysterious about the blast at the Washburn A Mill, the largest mill in the United States at the time, being blown apart in seconds. First of all, it was a flour mill. Secondly, there were no signs of malicious activity. The explosion in Minneapolis, Minnesota, on May 2, 1878, was so great that houses across the city shook and people thought they experienced an earthquake. The devastating blast, which occurred shortly after 7 p.m., was heard as far as St. Paul, a neighboring city about ten miles away. A gigantic fireball, eyewitnesses say, appeared in the evening sky as the seven-story mill erupted after the thunderous boom. The blast was so strong that debris from the mill was sent hundreds of feet into the air, scattering fiery fragments all over the surrounding area.

What caused the blast? No one knew. Nobody ever imagined that a flour mill could explode like that. The mystery was intensified because no explosive materials were detected in the mill factory. People were stumped at the strange phenomenon except for two professors at the nearby University of Minnesota who suspected flour—the very thing that was in front of everyone—could cause the blast. Flour? People laughed it off as a ludicrous idea.

The professors conducted controlled experiments and proved that flour—specifically, flour dust—caused the explosion. Not only that, they also identified how the giant flour mill had all the necessary conditions to create such a huge explosion. In addition, they mentioned what sparked the explosion. The flour mill used two giant millstones to grind the grain into powder. As the world's largest flour mill, the A Mill produced enormous amounts of flour dust. Furthermore, the factory had little ventilation which meant that dust particles were trapped in a confined, tightly compacted space.

The fact that the seven-story mill had huge indoor space meant more oxygen interacted with the flour dust, which was a critical component in making flour dust combustible. As shocking as it may sound, flour dust, combined with the right conditions and factors, is more explosive than gunpowder. The pressurized chamber was ripe for combustion and all that was needed was a spark from the millstones. The explosion occurred after the day shift ended at 6 p.m. The time between shift meant that the millstones were running dry, causing sparks to fly when they rubbed against each other. As news spread that flour dust caused the explosion, people were amazed that food can potentially combust. How could flour, an ordinary, common kitchen ingredient found in every cupboard, explode?

Similarly, holy combustions ignite people in the same way. It is the moment of internal eruption caused by a combination of pressure and buildup that releases a powerful reaction. The encounter with Jesus triggers the combustion itself.

Combustion is the moment of joy and release that one feels after a genuine encounter. There is the first combustion after meeting Jesus but individuals can have ongoing series of combustions throughout their lives. One of the expressions of holy combustion is joy, like the "unbridled horse" feeling that Dr. Pati Graham felt.

The word *combustion* may be the last word that comes to mind when thinking about evangelism. Combustion suggests ignition, flame, or fire. Sometimes a fire burns out quickly and dies. On the other hand, a great fire grows in intensity and can spread to outlying areas. In this and the following chapter, we will see that combustion doesn't involve strategy, money, committee approval, or volunteers. When God enables combustion, it leads to a holy combustion within people that demands to be released.

The fire at Sumo Sushi and the explosion at Washburn Mill are examples of combustions in action and the ripple effect that followed. The incidents at a sushi restaurant and a flour mill sound like they have little in common but share an underlying pattern. First of all, a tiny spark was all that was needed to start the combustion. In freestyle evangelism, the spark is the Holy Spirit. When people encounter Jesus, a holy combustion erupts from within, causing a spiritual explosion that transforms the individual. Freestyle evangelism cannot succeed without the Holy Spirit because the Holy Spirit is the One who enables the holy combustion to take place.

The second distinguishing characteristic of these two examples is that combustions had big effects in both cases. Had the sprinkler system not been activated, the fire started by the tempera flakes would have likely burned the restaurant down. The flour mill flattened the entire city block. A holy combustion in people is only the beginning. It can have life-changing effects. The fire is ignited within people and God's design is for the fire to spread.

Finally, both combustions happened spontaneously and unpredictably. No one saw them coming. The combustion came without warning. Workers at Sumo Sushi were laying out the tempura flakes as they normally did countless times before. Mill workers for the evening shift were coming in for the regular workday when the explosion occurred. What happened is that unforeseeable conditions, unbeknownst to people, were coming together that were ripe for a combustion. Similarly, we do not know when a holy combustion could erupt.

If we read the Gospels through the lens of combustion, Jesus was setting off holy combustions wherever he went, much to the sneering disapproval of Pharisees and religious officials who were aghast at the mess Jesus was making wherever he went. What they prized over all else was strict observance of all the religious rules and calling out anyone who fell out of line. Not only did Jesus not pay attention to the things they deeply cared about, but the combustions that Jesus was setting off did not look like religion. The Pharisees saw little in what Jesus did that aligned with what they promoted and reinforced.

Principle of Restraint

In enabling combustion to happen, we allow it to ignite and help it spread. This is the principle of restraint in freestyle evangelism. It guides our thinking about how God is working in a situation and not taking steps that would hinder or stop the Holy Spirit. How do we stop the Holy Spirit? There are many ways to deter the Holy Spirit but the one obvious way is to make evangelism so defined, managed, and regulated that little or no room is made available for the Holy Spirit. When we practice restraint, we implicitly understand that we are not the primary agents in freestyle evangelism.

Think for a moment about the kind of person that comes to mind when I mention "evangelist." Many of you are probably thinking of a preacher who is a powerful orator. Take, for example, the parable that is often associated with evangelism. In the parable, someone goes out and scatters seeds and the seeds land on four different soils: road, rocky, with thorns, and fertile (Matthew 13:3–8, Mark 4:3–8, Luke 8:5–8). You probably know which parable I am referring to. What do we call that parable? What would we say is the important person or thing in that parable? If you thought

"Parable of the Sower," that is what most of us think the parable is about. We presume the sower—the preacher, pastor, evangelist, gifted speaker, church scholar or official—to be the main figure in evangelism.

The principle of restraint helps to prevent us from idolizing a preacher, evangelist, or a strategy when God should receive the glory. The issue of exalting a Christian leader was central to a major commotion in 1 Corinthians, chapter 3 that Paul felt he needed to address. In the chapter, Paul was very upset with the Corinthians. What got Paul so mad? Paul says, "For when one [in the Corinthian church] says, 'I belong to Paul', and another, 'I belong to Apollos', are you not merely human (v. 4)?"

Bragging about how their Christian leader was superior led to "jealousy" and "quarreling" among Christians. In deep disappointment, Paul rebuked them and called them a "people of the flesh" (v. 1). Paul expresses surprise that they haven't *yet* matured in faith. "Even now you are still not ready," Paul says, "for you are still of the flesh" (vv. 2–3). Are you not "behaving according to human inclinations" (v. 3)? Paul asks. The verse (v. 3) in the Amplified version reads: "You are still worldly [controlled by ordinary impulses, the sinful capacity]. For as long as there is jealousy and strife and discord among you, are you not unspiritual, and are you not walking like ordinary men [unchanged by faith]?"

Paul very much wishes he could reveal more substantial teaching to them "as spiritual people," but he cannot because they are "not ready for solid food" (vv. 1–2). Their understanding of the faith remains at the surface level. As a result, Paul could only feed them "milk" since they are "infants in Christ" (vv. 1–2). Paul implores the Corinthians to stop this sort of celebrity Christianity. "What then is Apollos? What is Paul?" (v. 5), Paul asks in amazement.

Freestyle as Self-Propelled Evangelism

One of the most striking facts about holy combustions—which can happen when you least expect it—is that it produces an innate desire to make Jesus known to those around you. This possibility of self-propelled evangelism, which the Holy Spirit initiates, is at the center of the idea of freestyle and might well be difficult to accept. The combustion ignited within individuals is so strong that it generates energy that must be released. No external prompting is needed; it moves on its own. Think about the holy combustion that the Samaritan woman and Zacchaeus experienced.

The Samaritan woman came to the well at noon, an indication that she wanted to be left alone. People came in the morning to draw water for the rest of the day but it also served as a social event. The women would gather at the well and, as each took their turn, catch up with one another, update neighbors on the latest news of what was happening with their families, and, perhaps, share the latest gossip in town. They checked up on each other if one of them was going through something. After all, they had all known each other their whole lives, but, for this particular Samaritan woman, she avoided her community.

She deliberately came at noon knowing full well that the last of the women who wanted water would have left. And noon was the perfect time before the start of those who would come early in the late afternoon to draw water for the evening, such as the scene in Genesis 24:10–14, when Abraham's servant finally reached Rebekah's town. He made his camels kneel by the well "while it was toward evening, the time when women go out to draw water" (v. 11).

By coming to the well at noon, she picked the perfect time when no one would be there—or, so she thought. As she approached the well, she was startled to see a man. Right away, she could tell he was Jewish by his appearance, and he started to talk to her and ask for a drink. She was stunned that a Jew would ask her for a drink. Such instances did not happen since touching anything Samaritan would render them unclean. When Jesus asked for a drink of water, it meant that Jesus would touch the same bucket or vessel that she used to give him a drink. In addition, during that era, talking with any woman in public (who was not from his family) was highly unconventional. When Jesus's disciples later arrived on the scene, they were "astonished that he was speaking with a woman" (John 4:27).

If his disciples returned earlier, Jesus's encounter with the Samaritan woman might have happened very differently but the conversation at the well was between Jesus and her, a Jewish man and a Samaritan woman, two ethnic groups with an intense dislike for each other. Even though passing through Samaria was the quickest route from Jerusalem to Galilee, some Jews preferred to walk around Samaria to avoid walking on Samaritan ground. However, on this particular journey, Jesus chose to stop at the well.

Jesus sent his disciples ahead to buy food and supplies while he rested at the well alone. It was about noon, the hottest time of the day. Jesus wanted some water but there was no vessel or bucket to draw water. This was not unusual. Locals brought their own drawing vessel to the well to prevent others from taking their water.[30] It could be animal skins sewn together like the one Hagar used in Genesis 21:19. With God's guidance, Hagar discovered a well and "filled the skin with water." In the case of the Samaritan woman, she brought a water jar to the well, a scene similar to Rebekah coming to the well "with her water jar upon her shoulder" (Genesis 24:15). The water jar would be tied to a rope and lowered into the well to be filled.

In Rebekah's story, Abraham's servant asked her for water. Rebekah "lowered her jar upon her hand and gave him a drink" (Genesis 24:18). After she generously gave him more than enough to drink, Rebekah didn't stop there. She said, "I will draw for your camels also, until they have finishing drinking" (v. 19). When you consider that Abraham's servant had *ten* camels and thirsty camels can drink up to fifty-three gallons in three minutes, Rebekah's kindness was extraordinary. She poured water into the trough and "ran again [and again] to the well to draw, and she drew for all his camels" (v. 20).

Jesus wasn't as fortunate when he asked for a drink. Instead of a generous helping of water, he received a snappy retort: "How is that you, a Jew, ask a drink of me, a woman of Samaria?" (John 4:9). She wasn't about to give Jesus a drink, even though she could probably tell he was exhausted and thirsty. She became argumentative, aggressive even, and started to pull Jesus into a heated discussion over the ethnic strife that has cursed the relationship between Jews and Samaritans for too long.

Even though she rejected Jesus's request, that did not stop Jesus as he saw her and had compassion. Jesus knew why she came to the well at noon. Jesus knew about her troubled personal life that she hid under her tough exterior. She came to the well for water but she came away with "living water." Jesus used "water" to first talk about drinking water but later, as a metaphor, to engage her weary soul. Jesus in a blunt manner reveals how her personal life has been left parched to which Jesus offers her "living water."

She experiences holy combustion. What she does next is unimaginable. For someone who deliberately avoided people and secluded herself like a self-imposed exile from her community, she acted out of character. In an excited, hyped-up manner, she runs through the city streets, like a loud, revivalist preacher, proclaiming loudly to whoever within an earshot. She grabs people in the streets, runs into people's houses, and hollers across the marketplace. She is animated, full of emotion and jubilation.

She could not help herself but to release Jesus. A holy combustion creates that kind of energy. Her desire to witness to them was irrepressible. The townspeople were astonished.

What could have made her *this* excited? She was running around town like an unbridled horse, released and ecstatic. She was the last person the townspeople expected to be an outspoken evangelist but that was exactly why people believed her. She was authentic. It was completely spontaneous. It flowed out naturally and was real and genuine.

Her evangelistic effect on her city was so strong that the entire city became abuzz about this Jesus who got her so excited. People stopped what they were doing, "left the city and were on their way to" see Jesus. It is not hard to imagine that her passionate outpouring was why people believed in her testimony. Because of her, "many Samaritans from that city believed in [Jesus] because of the woman's testimony" (John 4:39). Many were led to Christ as a result of her holy combustion. Because of her, the whole city got to hear about Jesus and "many more believe because of his word" (v. 41).

The Samaritan woman's evangelism is one of the most extraordinary examples of spontaneous reactions after encountering Jesus, but you never got the sense that "doing" evangelism was her intention. Her evangelism was less about proclaiming Jesus than sharing an amazing encounter that she wanted everyone to know about. She would tell you that she doesn't know systematic theology or biblical studies but she would tell you with conviction that she knows Jesus firsthand and Jesus has transformed her. In other words, her actions were not how we, today, think about evangelism—a conscious and deliberate activity of doing evangelism. She was simply being herself. In fact, she gave little thought to how her wild display of enthusiasm might run the risk of being judged or looked down upon. There's certainly a risk that goes with expressing your unbridled joy that makes Christians question if it's appropriate to show such jubilation in the church.

Zacchaeus the Chief Tax Collector

Zacchaeus, the "wee little man" that we learned about in Sunday school, was in the tax collecting business, but he was not an ordinary tax collector. He was a *chief* tax collector. Tax collection was dirty work, and tax collectors were seen as being the worst. People openly despised tax collectors and people were aghast that Jesus would associate himself with them. In Mark 2:16, the Pharisees asked the disciples, "Why does your teacher eat with tax-collectors and sinners?" They could not believe that a man of piety should ever be seen interacting with one, let alone dining with them.

Jesus used the hatred to mirror what was in their hearts. In many instances, Jesus used tax collectors to illustrate key lessons. Jesus asked, "If you love those who love you, what reward do you have? Do not even the tax collectors do the same?" (Matthew 5:46). In other words, are you not doing the same thing as tax collectors? Don't presume, Jesus warns his listeners, that you are better than a tax collector. Jesus said, "Truly I tell you, the tax collector and the prostitutes are going into the kingdom of God ahead of you" (Matthew 21:31). In the Parable of the Pharisee and the Tax Collector (Luke 18:9–14), Jesus shamed the self-righteousness of a religious leader by contrasting him with a humble, repentant tax collector.

Things happened in a hurry after Jesus spotted Zacchaeus in a sycamore tree. Zacchaeus escorted Jesus to his house where he threw a lavish party but not everyone was happy. "All who saw it began to grumble and said, 'He [Jesus] had gone to be the guest of one who is a sinner [Zacchaeus]'" (v. 7). Nevertheless, encountering Jesus ignited a holy combustion in Zacchaeus, just like the one the Samaritan woman experienced at the well and ended up stunning everyone in the mansion with a wild proclamation. In a loud voice so that everyone could hear his promise, Zacchaeus declared, "Look, half of my possessions, Lord, I will give to the poor; and if I have defrauded anyone of anything, I will pay back four times as much" (v. 8). Everyone could not believe their ears.

How did this happen? How did Zacchaeus and the Samaritan woman become amazing evangelists? By any measure, their evangelism was compelling and awe-inspiring, but neither was trying to do evangelism in the sense of deliberately doing evangelism. Yet, somehow, that's exactly what they did. They were praising Jesus to everyone precisely because the irrepressible urge to make Christ known bubbled over from the inside out. In other words, they were being themselves.

Evangelism as Authentic Expression

Everything Zacchaeus and the Samaritan woman did that made their evangelistic witness such a huge success falls outside our notions of evangelism. Christians don't have the words to describe what happened to them, other than to say they had a radical conversion. However, the texture of their evangelism was substantially different: It was spontaneous, thrilling, passionate, individualized, and authentic. As we have seen from their combustion, passion is infectious. In other words, when people observe us doing something with passion and enjoyment, they see authenticity. Authentic responses to Jesus can't be manufactured.

This is an important distinction. If we think about evangelism this way—as focused on "Christ in me" and not on changing the other person—it is possible to understand how unscripted, authentic expressions of Christ can have enormous impact. When Christ becomes the main point of our expression, our passion for Christ comes through and he is far more contagious than anything we can ever do.

The holy combustion started with the Samaritan woman and Zacchaeus but it quickly spread. For the Samaritan woman, her community was the entire city. Everyone knew her. For Zacchaeus, his closest people were fellow tax collectors. The movement that the Samaritan woman and Zacchaeus started didn't have a leader or any kind of organization. It happened organically. Then it grew like wildfire. Just as those standing near a small explosion feel its effects, those near a holy combustion also experience the residual impact as the authentic movement of the Holy Spirit reverberates around the action.

Evangelism that encourages holy combustions is a very different kind of evangelism from the ministry we think and practice. Freestyle evangelism is self-initiated and self-propelling as its power is generated by holy combustions. Leaning on the self-propelling energy that combustions provide, freestyle upends the top-down model and pushes against the constraints of linear evangelism.

CHAPTER THREE

Examples of Holy Combustions

Sometimes, combustions happen when we don't expect it, like the fire at Sumo Sushi and explosion at Washburn Mills. At other times, we expect combustions but they don't quite happen as we thought. That is because combustible elements are unique to individuals, peoples, subcultures, and nations. Combustions reveal the traits that they already possess and empower people to take them to express Jesus.

This chapter will examine examples of holy combustions and its aftereffects. The institutional church tends to operate in a predictable and organized fashion but holy combustions break through and enlarges individuals' sense of perceived limits. It injects a jolt of confidence that can alter one's idea of what can be achieved. When holy combustions happen, an individual releases a burst of energy, and evangelism is the outward expression of the individual's reorientation in Christ.

Just as obscure elements such as tempura flakes and flour dust can combust, the way combustions occur are virtually limitless. It can happen at any age, background, occupation, and subculture. Consider "Bee Party," an event that Pastor In

Yong Lee and Chele Mills, a lay member of Pastor Lee's church, organized as their project after the evangelism conference.

Pastor Lee turned to Mills, an unlikely person for an evangelism project. If you meet her, she comes across as a quiet, soft-spoken, and gentle person. A self-described introvert, speaking in public is the last thing on her mind, but Pastor Lee saw something in her. She knew she loves Jesus but Pastor Lee wanted to know more about her. She discovered that she loves bees and is a certified beekeeper.

She suggested a Bee Party where Mills could lead a group of people interested in honeybees. At first, Mills was taken aback. She admittedly was "nervous." In addition, she wasn't sure if she was the right person for the job. She says, "I am a newbie beekeeper having only become certified and having my first hives this year."

As it turned out, the Bee Party was the right kind of evangelism for her. When I spoke with her, Mills mentioned how she wanted to be a missionary when she was younger but hates the kind of Christianity that "pushes the Bible" down on people. Her motto is to "preach the gospel without words." The Bee Party was simply an opportunity for people with like-minded passion for bees to come together. That's it. No mention of religion or church attendance or any other hidden agenda.

Pastor Lee and Mills set the party for 2 p.m. on December 15, 2022. They didn't know how well (or badly) this was going to go. No one had done this before. Twelve people showed up for the party, half from the congregation and the others nonmembers. Pastor Lee started the party with introductions and then Mills allowed people in the room to share their passion. They were surprised to learn that half of the people there were either current beekeepers or were beekeepers at one point, or helped family members who were beekeepers.

In the beginning, people did not know each other but, at a certain point, there was a spark, a palpable energy that they observed erupting at the party. Mills observed how the vibe in the room became "very pleasant" and "dynamic." She said, "It was a very positive experience for me. I was thoroughly impressed with the way they treated me and one another." Pastor Lee said, "No one was monopolizing. Everyone enjoyed it. It was amazing."

They passionately discussed bees, their significance to society, and how they need us to survive. They enthusiastically shared insights about the honeybees' intelligence in communicating with each other. They shared where to get the best local honey and the differences between store-brand and locally produced honey. They picked each other's brains about beekeeping tips, such as expenses, room required to keep bees, and bee sting allergies. They shared recipes such as oatmeal cookies using vanilla infused with fresh honey.

Time flew and Mills had to reluctantly stop the party. Pastor Lee observed, "It was so good. Everything went so smoothly and spontaneously. The entire group participated in it with such joy and interest." She laughed and said, "It was fun to watch." What happened at the Bee Party was a release of powerfully attractive authenticity. Pastor Lee said, "They went on and on. Nonstop for two hours." People told Mills how much they enjoyed it and "would love to meet with the group again." What was interesting was that people wanted to get back together, and it didn't need to be about bees. They yearned for authentic human connection that this one-time event delivered.

Holy combustions are important for more than simply igniting a spark. Once holy combustions happen, their influence has a ripple effect. Granted, the Bee Party's combustion seems small but it is a mistake to think that a small one cannot trigger a bigger one or lead to more combustion. Combustions in whatever shape or form reverberate in the spiritual landscape, influencing people in ways we cannot fully comprehend.

What happened at the Bee Party shares basic underlying patterns with other combustions. First of all, it is an example of an authentic expression. Pastor Lee made sure that the Bee Party had no agenda or obligations. No one felt the pressure of expectations of any kind, other than to simply connect with one another through the joy of bees and beekeeping. In essence, they created an environment that enabled people to be themselves.

One of the things that Pastor Lee noticed while preparing for the Bee Party was how invitations to church activities make people wary. She said,

> When a church wants to ask people to gather as a group, they are suspicious because they are tired of

seeing churches pretending to do something when all they want is to bring them into their churches. When it is clear that you are not planning to do that at all and the event itself is it. That is the deal. And just having that event and having a good time and fellowship. We can give people a good impression, a good image of our church.

The second distinguishing characteristic is that the combustion has an element of uncertainty. If your evangelism project is carefully planned, neatly organized, and orderly, then there's little or no room for anything else to happen. Risk is built into freestyle evangelism. Jesus took a risk by inviting himself to the home of the chief tax collector, bringing heaps of criticism upon himself. "*All* [emphasis mine] who saw it began to grumble and said, '[Jesus] has gone to be the guest of one who is a sinner [Zacchaeus]'" (Luke 19:7). Jesus ran the risk of causing his disciples to question him when he spoke to the Samaritan woman at the well. When the disciples returned to the well and found Jesus having a conversation with her, they were "astonished", but "no one said, 'What do you want?' or, 'Why are you speaking with her?'" (John 4:27).

Finally, the combustion happened in a hurry. Mills said it was as if a light switch turned on during the Bee Party when the mood abruptly changed. When we freestyle and share Jesus with people with no agenda or expectation, we invite the Holy Spirit into the mix. The "risk" element in freestyle evangelism is actually stepping out to "walk by faith" (2 Corinthians 5:7). In order to "walk by faith, not by sight," we suspend our own understanding or experiences and trust in

God's leading even when we might feel unsure—a task that is not as easy as it appears. When you freestyle, you are not sure how it will work out. You may not be sure if anything will work but you trust that God will deliver you.

When we step out in faith, it is like calling out to God for leadership. When we cede control, we invite God's intervention in our evangelism, and we may be surprised by what we find. Jesus described the unexpected happenings in the Parable of the Growing Seed (Mark 4:26–27):

> The kingdom of God is as if someone would scatter seed on the ground, and would sleep and rise night and day, and the seed would sprout and grow, he does not know how.

One woman enjoyed the Bee Party so much that she gave Pastor Lee a handmade thank-you card. At the follow-up meeting, Pastor Lee brought the card with her and showed the group the beautiful card that was intricately made with a bee and honeycomb design. Pastor Lee was so amazed to see her hidden, beautiful talent that it sparked the idea to branch off to start a "Hand-Made Card Party." Pastor Lee asked her if she would be interested in leading the meeting if an event was organized around card-making. She replied, "Sure!"

These three characteristics—one, commitment to authenticity; two, acceptance of risk and uncertainty; and three, that holy combustion happens with the invitation of the Holy Spirit—limit our intervention in evangelism. Freestyle evangelism restrains the human urge to control and manage the situation. Of the three, the third trait—the idea that God needs to be included in our evangelism efforts as an active co-partner—is the most important, because combustions cannot start without a spark and God is the one who ignites. We can bring piles of the finest fire-burning wood and barrels of fuel but nothing will happen without a spark.

See You at the Pole

In early 1990, a small group of Christian teens from the Fort Worth suburb of Burleson, Texas, attended a weekend youth retreat. This retreat had a powerful impact on the youth. On Saturday night, "their hearts were penetrated like never before, when they became broken before God and burdened for their friends."[31] Their hearts burned with passion for their friends but they were unsure what to do.

They decided they should pray for their friends. That very night, ten of them drove to three different schools. They drove to the empty school parking lot, not knowing what to do next. They knew they had to pray for their friends. One of them suggested that they gather around the school flagpole. It seemed like a good idea. The flagpole was kind of a central meeting area. Standing around the pole, they prayed for their schools, friends, and leaders.

This group of Christian teens in the 1990s tried to find a way to express their hearts before God. But then, without warning, the act became a phenomenon and a prayer movement was started. This was the birth of "See You at the Pole."

Youth leaders across Texas heard of what these youngsters did and encouraged other Christian youth nationwide to meet at the flagpole and pray. The vision was promoted to youth groups across the state. There was no sign-up or reservations. They told the youth to come to their flagpole at 7 a.m. on September 12, 1990. Considering that this was a time before the Internet and social media, the event was broadcast by word of mouth. The event relied on teens waking earlier than usual before school to pray, which is no small feat. No one was exactly sure how it would turn out but somehow the news of the event spread to nearby states and, when the day came, it is estimated that more than forty-five thousand teens, in four different states, met to pray at their school flagpoles.

The movement caught fire. Youth pastors around the country heard of what happened. An unofficial national day of prayer was started and it was organized and led by students. They were encouraged to do it again the following year. A date was set, September 11, 1991 at 7 a.m. An estimated one million students across the country, from Boston to Los Angeles, gathered around the flagpole to pray. There was nothing elaborate about it. They gathered around the flagpole, prayed for their leaders and country, and concluded.

Now, "See You at the Pole" has become an annual global event held on the fourth Wednesday in September. Students have gathered around the pole to pray in more than sixty-four countries, such as Ivory Coast, Korea, Canada, Japan, and Turkey. In 2023, at a high school in Russellville, Arkansas, over eighty students gathered for "See You at the Pole" but that wasn't the only day Christian students gathered. For the past year, students gathered "every morning" to pray.[32] A youth who witnessed the prayer movement said, "It was truly awesome to be around a group of high schoolers from a variety of local youth ministries who love Jesus and through whom God is moving and to get to know many of these students and see their heart for Jesus and for their friends."[33]

These days, teenagers are not the only ones meeting at the pole. Elementary school children gathered around the flagpole at White Hall Elementary School.[34] Remarkably, the children got their parents to pray along with them. Parents dropping off their kids watched; some stood at a distance and prayed. Children and teens, when given the space and opportunity to flex their evangelism, can surprise us all.

Ninety-Five-Year-Old Ruth Spence

Ruth Spence's evangelism is not your typical evangelism. She is not fond of public speaking or leading people in ministry. She does however love to quilt. The ninety-five-year-old Spence says, "I still just love to sew. Make quilts. Love it. And I still love to sew… for someone else."[35] Notice that she said "love" three times. Freestyle evangelism is about doing what you love and combining your love and passions with Jesus. In Spence's case, she loves to quilt and expresses that love to people as an expression of her faith.

Quilting may not be what we would call evangelism, but for Spence and many others, it is their "stroke" to express Jesus to the world. By 2014, Spence had made seventy-seven quilts for the Quilts of Valor Foundation. Seventy-seven may not seem like much over the decades but when you consider that one quilt can take as much as six months or longer to make you begin to realize her level of commitment. She was first introduced to Quilts of Valor by her church.

What is Quilts of Valor? It's an organization whose mission is "to cover service members and veterans touched by war with comforting and healing quilts of valor."[36] These quilts are not given to just anyone. Individual soldiers need to be nominated and accepted to receive a quilt. Each quilt is handmade and "awarded" to individual soldiers who have witnessed combat.

Healing is the central idea of Quilts of Valor and the fact that each quilt has been individually handcrafted by someone lends particular comfort to those who have witnessed war and combat. Ruth Spence in particular feels for the soldiers who "don't come home well."[37] Imagine you are a battle-scarred soldier. You've seen horrific things on the battlefield that you're probably keeping to yourself. You may be suffering from physical injuries and/or PTSD. And you receive a handwoven quilt made just for you as a token of gratitude for your service. You find out that Ruth Spence lovingly prayed over the quilt while stitching it over many months to recognize your service and cover you in comfort. Even though recipients of her quilts won't get a chance to meet her, Ruth Spence's heart is stitched onto all of her quilts. How did she develop such a big heart for them? Many of Spence's family members served in the military. "I had six brothers in World War II," Spence says, "and they all came home."[38]

People may say her work isn't evangelism. It's certainly not what you'd typically think as evangelism. A religious tract was not handed out. A salvation message was not preached. However, love and compassion were delivered; that is enough for many people. Freestyle evangelism doesn't have to be flashy; it recognizes the atypical gifts, passions, and callings of people. Freestyle broadens our narrow understanding of evangelism and will activate a greater participation of ordinary, unassuming people in the pews. A large swath of the Christian population remains untapped because of our mindset of what evangelism should look like. Freestyle evangelism is about releasing people in their own way and enabling them to make an impact for Christ. "It's giving and doing," Spence said. "I've gotten a lot more than I've given, and I've given a lot." Of the five hundred plus quilts she has made over her lifetime, the vast majority have been "for other people."

Drums and Church Growth

In 1980, an American church delegation visited Africa and learned of the surprising growth of Christianity throughout sub-Saharan Africa. Church officials wanted to know what was spurring the dramatic rise of Christianity. Perhaps they thought they could bring some of their ideas back to the US where churches have been declining for decades.

African church leaders cited an unusual reason. They didn't mention church projects or new evangelism initiatives. Rather, the growth resulted from "Africanizing" their churches "with music and story."[39] Specifically, church leaders in West Africa and Zaire told the Americans, "We started to grow when the drums came in the church."[40]

Is evangelism that simple? Africanize the church to Africans? Germanize to Germans? Koreanize to Koreans? Cubanize to Cubanos? African Americanize to African Americans? Partly. At the beginning of the twentieth century, when missionaries introduced the gospel to Africa, they prevented Africans from using their drums and music in the church because they were deemed foreign elements in the church. Missionaries came to Africa with a particular set of ideas about what Christianity should look and sound like and African drums were not a part of that vision.

If, however, missionaries were to Africanize Christianity for Africans, what would that look like? More likely than not, the results would look very different from what Africans would do themselves to Africanize Christianity. The key point is that people in an ethnic culture or subculture have superior cultural insight into what ignites their people. Because they are privy to their group's cultural sensibilities, they instinctively understand what themes and elements resonate powerfully from the inside out.

Enabling people in subcultures to reimagine the church would be an eye-opening experiment. Imagine what the church would look like if a group of avid Christian skateboarders infused their distinctive lifestyle and artistic expression to skateboardize the church? Or, imagine assigning a group of Gen Z social media Christian influencers to Gen Z the church? Or, imagine assigning a group of Christian convicts who served long sentences to re-envision the church? Or, imagine assigning a group of rabid college football fans to refashion the church with their unique passion? If, by chance, these passionate college football fans had the opportunity to immerse the church in their subculture, newcomers who are also passionate college football fans would feel an instant, authentic connection as if they felt "This is where I belong." The same would be true for skateboarders, Gen Zers, and convicts who would recognize themselves in the environment and feel familiar vibes. Once again, the important distinction is that the output is not manufactured or contrived in any way but is a natural extension of the ethnic culture or subculture.

Seventeen-Year-Old Nancy Jang

In 1977, a seventeen-year-old Korean American, Nancy Jang penned a letter to the regional church newspaper about an important personal matter.[41] She acknowledged that she struggled with an identity crisis. She asked herself, "Who am I?" As an ethnic minority growing up in New Jersey, she wrestled with her sense of self. Born to Korean immigrants, Jang was very Americanized at the same time and wasn't sure if what she was doing was the right step in her identity formation. "Trying to know myself," Jang wrote, "became a difficult, confusing task. I did not know where and how to begin."[42]

Jang learned about the Declaration of Independence, Civil War, and American civic responsibilities but hardly anything about her own culture and traditions. After some soul-searching, Jang said, "[I] came up with the realization that I do not truly know anything of my Korean heritage."[43] Her trouble was not a surprise. Growing up in the suburbs of New Jersey, "I have forgotten," Jang wrote, "the language that I used to speak so well, I do not know any of the history that formed Korea and finally I have forgotten a major part of Korean culture and traditions."[44] In the end, her life journey up to that point, Jang admitted, "eliminated the Korean side of me" which left her feeling "isolated."[45] Jang began to realize is that her ethnicity wasn't a barrier to Jesus. In fact, she found a pathway for self-discovery in her ethnic culture and Korean church.

Denise Cuesta

Ethnic cultures and subcultures help connect people to themselves and God. Consider Denise Cuesta, a Puerto Rican Christian living in New York City. She remembers how her church disapproved of ethnic culture in the church, making sure that it wasn't seen out in the open. She says, "The major thing was a feeling that my culture was sinful. It was wrong to try to be cultural or to try to bring my cultural perspective into my faith. Christianity had to be separate from all of that or somehow above all of that. Culture was worldly and Christianity was heavenly."[46]

As an adult and mother, Cuesta looks back to see how the church's approach has disconnected her from her ethnic culture. She remained steadfast to Jesus and church but without the support of her cultural roots.

Now that she has gotten older, she wonders about her experience and whether this approach was right. No matter how she dissects the situation, she grows frustrated over not having her ethnic culture an integral part of her Christian faith. She asks, "The gospel has to be more than this one-dimensional spiritual life. I can't assume anymore that God's not interested in what I do and how I live."[47]

Cuesta grew up with a large extended family and Thanksgiving is always a time for everyone to get together. It's a blast for all the adults, and all the cousins as well, to be together in one place. On one Thanksgiving weekend, everyone was having a good time, and she witnessed an adorable moment with her daughter. Members of her husband's family were showing her how to dance salsa.

Watching her do the salsa steps, she saw her daughter's eyes glimmer as she immersed herself in Latino culture. A sudden moment of awareness hit Cuesta. She says,

> I realize I never had that and felt a void, a sense of loss of never having had it. I had never been allowed to feel a sense of belonging not only to God's family but to my Latino community. I miss the sense of the strong Latino family unit, the ties and the acceptance of extended family.[48]

Never had she considered dance as acceptable in the Christian faith. She says, "In the past I was very resistant to using dance as a form of worship because I did not see it emphasized in the White church."[49]

The experience of growing up in church "culture-free" was difficult and disconcerting. But it's not just about the absence of culture. It's bigger than that. It touches and affects larger self-image, belonging, community, and identity issues. Cuesta says, "I am discovering that if I don't know who I am in the context of culture, then I don't really know who I am."[50] She is also concerned that the disconnect with ethnic culture may unsettle her relationship with God in some way. "That has to affect my relationship with God," she added. "I have adopted ways of thinking and attitudes that are in line with majority White culture instead of Latino culture."[51]

For Nancy Jang, she discovered her identity and Jesus at the same place: her Korean church where she found answers to "all these things."[52] It's a development that shows us how ethnic churches can tackle the sort of big, philosophical questions raised by diverse peoples and how seamlessly Jang combined her spiritual pursuits with concerns often pushed aside as secular or unrelated to spiritual formation. Fortunately for Jang, she rediscovered the language she "had once known" at her church. Church members were kind and generous with their time in sharing key elements of their traditions and heritage and helped "piece together many of the past historical events of Korean history."

The nagging unease has given way to a deeply felt awareness of herself and the contributing factors to that awareness; the feelings of rootlessness have given way to a keen appreciation of the tangled complexities of the mind, heart, and spirit. The critical thing that she learned from her ethnic church was, according to Jang, "I am proud to be a Korean and I am proud of my heritage. These Korean people [in the church] are not less American than other Americans living here. But as in all ethnic groups, there exists another identity."[53]

As Jang is explaining her new sense of self, the seventeen-year-old is aware of her critics. They may wonder about her Americanness, and whether she is withdrawing from the larger society in pursuit of a tribal community. In anticipation of such questions, Jang said,

> Learning about my Korean culture does not mean I am going to abandon my American way of life. It is too precious a discovery to abandon. Therefore, I should like to make the best of both worlds—my own native Korean heritage and the environment of my adopted country.[54]

Freestyle as a Family Affair

After experiencing holy combustion, the first group of people they tend to share the news with is their community. It's not a conscious decision. They instinctively turn to their family, friends, and subculture. In Mark 2:13–15, Jesus walks along the shores of the Sea of Galilee with "the whole crowd gathered around him" when he sees Levi, a tax collector, working in a tax booth. Jesus calls out to Levi, "Follow me," and Levi leaves the tax booth to join Jesus. When Levi hosts Jesus for dinner, "many tax-collectors and sinners were also sitting with Jesus" (v. 15). Levi's livelihood was tax collecting and his circle of friends was also in the same profession. Similarly, we can imagine when Jesus called down Zacchaeus from the sycamore tree and had dinner at Zacchaeus's house, tax collectors and "sinners" also joined the feast.

When good things happen to you or you discover a hidden gem, our inclination is to tell our closest people about it and this includes encountering Jesus. When Andrew encountered Jesus in John 1:40–41, who did he share Jesus with? Andrew "first found his brother Simon and said to him, 'We have found the Messiah.'" Andrew took it a step further and "brought Simon to Jesus." In Acts 16, Paul and Silas encountered a group of women while looking for a place of prayer near a river outside Philippi's city gate. They shared the gospel with them and Lydia, a businesswoman who traded purple cloth, believed in the good news and excitedly shared Jesus with her family who also believed. As a result, Lydia and "her household were baptized" (Acts 16:15).

While still in Philippi, Paul and Silas were "dragged into the market place before the authorities" and were arrested (Acts 16:19). They were subsequently stripped and "severely flogged," and imprisoned in jail with chains and stocks on their feet. About midnight, a violent earthquake shook the prison and immediately opened "all the doors." Miraculously everyone's chains were unfastened. Having seen the doors all open, the jailer assumed the worst and thought that the prisoners had escaped. He took out his sword and was about to kill himself before Paul spoke up, "Do not harm yourself, for we are all here" (Acts 16:28).

From this point onward, listen to how this became a family affair. After witnessing the supernatural events unfold, the jailer became eager to hear Paul and Silas. Never mind the fact that his job was supposed to keep them incarcerated. And now he was bringing these "accused criminals" to his home. Why? The jailer wanted his family to hear the gospel. It gets better. The jailer also didn't care that he was waking everyone up in his home in the middle of the night. He was just so excited, he *had* to wake them up.

He and his entire household believed and "he and his entire family were baptized without delay" (Acts 16:33). After he was baptized, he excitedly stood before them and expressed the joy of the Lord to them all. It was a thrilling moment for the entire family in the middle of the night as they all found Jesus together. "He and his entire household rejoiced that he had become a believe in Jesus" (Acts 16:34).

A Small Spark Can Start Big Fires

The scene was the 2022 Southwest Regional Championship game of the Little League World Series. On August 9, the game aired on ESPN between East Texas and Oklahoma. It was the first inning and Kaiden Shelton was pitching for East Texas. Although he got two outs, two were on base. He needed one more out and Isaiah Jarvis came to bat. Shelton worked fast and got two strikes on Jarvis. He wanted to throw a pitch inside but the ball got away from him and struck Jarvis in the head, making his helmet fly off. You could hear the crack of the helmet and gasps from the stands. Someone could be heard saying, "Oh my God!"

Jarvis fell to the ground. He held his head with both hands as he tossed and turned. Coaches rushed to Jarvis. Thankfully, he was alright. He got up, dusted himself off, and walked to first base. This is where things get interesting. After Jarvis walked to first base, he looked at Shelton on the pitcher's mound and approached him. Shelton thought the worst: "I thought he was going to throw a punch or something like that."[55]

What happened next turned into a viral sensation. After Jarvis took first base, he saw that Shelton was hurting—physically and emotionally. "I got to first base, and looked over at the pitcher and saw him with his glove on his face," Jarvis says, "I saw his face somehow, and could see he was crying so I dropped my helmet and went over there."[56] The move was spontaneous.

At that moment, Jarvis could have easily done nothing and let the game play on, which is what most of us would have done, but Jarvis did something extraordinary. Jarvis walks toward Shelton on the pitcher's mound, wraps his arms around him, hugs him, and says, "Hey, you're doing just great."[57] People who were shocked at first to see Jarvis get hit in the head were now stunned to witness such a heartwarming act. The stadium "erupted" in cheers; some fans started to cry.

Examples of Holy Combustions

What made Jarvis do what he did? It was a split-second decision. Jarvis felt the impulse, driven by faith, to act on behalf of someone he was uniquely able to help. In an interview, Jarvis said, "I wanted to go over there and spread God's love and make sure that he's OK, and make sure that he knows that I'm OK and that I'll be OK."[58] Jarvis could not bear the thought of Shelton carrying the weight of guilt and sought to release him from the burden. "If he didn't know I was OK," Jarvis said, "then he would be really down on himself and probably would not want to play the game anymore."[59] Jarvis's instincts proved correct. Shelton would later say, "I was scared because I thought I really hurt him and I thought I knocked him out. When he hugged me, it also made me feel amazing because...it showed me that he cared."[60]

They didn't know it at the time but the Internet, as they say, "blew up"—or, for this book, Jarvis freestyled and the situation combusted. Oklahoma ended up losing the game and, afterward, Coach took the boys out to eat. During dinner, he received a phone call from a producer of *Good Morning America*, the nationally aired ABC morning show. She wanted to talk to Jarvis about the video. Coach thought the producer was referring to Jarvis's amazing catch during the game. No, she was calling about the hug. The video of Jarvis hugging Shelton—only in a few hours—had gone "viral," according to the producer. It became so viral that the media could not ignore it. The producer said, "It's one of the most viral videos we've ever seen. It's gone wild."[61]

Good Morning America wasn't the only one calling. After the conversation, Coach received calls from *CBS Morning News*, *The New York Times*, *The Washington Post*, and ESPN. The situation was out of control. Because media outlets around the country kept calling, Coach put Jarvis in a booth at the restaurant to do "15 to 20 interviews."[62]

It didn't stop there. The story "got bigger and bigger" as Jarvis recalled. He began to get fan mail thanking him and expressing how his hug made a tremendous impact. People from across the country took time to pen letters about the difference he made. One letter said that he isn't a religious man, but his actions have brought the teachings of Jesus to life and made God more real to him. The Little League World Series president invited Jarvis and his family to Williamsport where he threw out the first pitch before the game between Texas and Hawaii. Jarvis did hours of interviews while he was there and adults were turning to the twelve-year-old for inspiration to which Jarvis replied, "It's crazy that adults kind of look up to me. It's kind of weird."[63]

Why did the hug go viral? Why this particular hug? Melody Shelton, Kaiden's mother, watched everything unfold in the stands and gave us a clue. She said, "I was in tears, like, I think all of us were pretty much crying at that point. At that moment, you realize that everything that you've been trying to teach your kids and that there's still good in the world—that was the moment between two twelve-year-olds."[64] For Jarvis, he didn't think of it much at the time. "It kind of felt like a natural reaction and I was just trying to spread God's love," Jarvis recalled.[65]

Needless to say, Jarvis would be the last to say that he is an evangelist or he did anything related to evangelism. He was just being himself. That is exactly the reason why it combusted. It was spontaneous, inspirational, and, most importantly, authentic. It was risky, but he walked out in faith and his gesture caught the world's attention. However, if you asked Jarvis, he would say he was simply living out his faith. Jarvis said, "Treat others how you want to be treated and put others before yourself."[66]

CHAPTER FOUR

Holy Combustions Happen in the Soil

When you look at the moon, what do you see? Perhaps you see a grayish, lifeless planetary satellite with thousands of craters. For researchers at NASA, they saw the moon differently. They saw potential for life. Starting in the 1960s, researchers conducted experiments to find the answer to a question about planetary life. The question is this: Can they grow plants and vegetables on the moon's soil? If so, what kind of food could they grow? Although these questions are fascinating on their own, they also led researchers to more questions. A professor at the University of Florida asked, "How might that [reality of fertile soil on the moon] one day help humans have an extended stay on the Moon."[67] A scientist with NASA goes a step further and suggests that the successful cultivation of plants on the moon "could provide supplemental nutrition to our diets and enable future human exploration."[68]

    The discovery of fertile soil on the moon would have far-reaching implications for exploring outer space and self-sustainability. According to a NASA administrator, the findings would promote "NASA's long-term human exploration goals as we'll need to use resources found on the

Moon and Mars to develop food sources for future astronauts living and operating in deep space."[69]

How did they get moon soil to conduct experiments? Researchers used the moon soil samples collected by astronauts from the Apollo 11, 12, and 17 missions. Researchers used rockcress (*Arabidopsis*) seeds to experiment and it wasn't by accident that they used rockcress seeds. Rockcress, which is related to cabbage and mustard, is a model organism to study plant biology. And more importantly, rockcress was the first plant to have its entire genome sequenced. As a result, researchers can carefully study the changes in the rockcress as it interacted with the moon soil, making it very useful.

At the NASA laboratories, they added water and seeds to small samples of moon soil. A nutrient solution was also regularly added. It's hard to imagine such an otherworldly idea working but that is exactly what happened. Much to their excitement, the seeds began to sprout after two days. A member of the research team said, "Everything sprouted. I can't tell you how astonished we were! Every plant—whether in a lunar sample or in a control—looked the same up until about day six."[70]

Then worrisome signs appeared after the sixth day. The plants stopped growing as well as they did earlier. While all of the samples showed remarkable growth in the first week, different samples exhibited varying degrees of health. The growth of some plants slowed, others showed stunted roots, some had reddish pigmentation, and others had stunted leaves.

The research team wanted to understand why they grew the way they did. After twenty days, they harvested the plants and ground them up to examine their RNA, the "control panel" of the DNA that carries out the biological processes. When they examined the sequencing of the RNA, they discovered something very surprising. The findings revealed the plants underwent high stress, as if they encountered a harsh environment. What was even more puzzling was that the moon soil samples collected from different Apollo missions produced different healthy results. Who could have imagined that moon rocks could actually support plant life?

While the researchers were enthusiastic about the growth of plants on moon soil, the experiments also raised more questions. How can they make moon soil less harsh and stressful for plants to grow? Are there variations of lunar soil in different parts of the moon?

Beach Soil

Here on Planet Earth, Joe Wilson is also trying to grow crops on different kinds of inhospitable soil. Wilson's farm is minutes from Myrtle Beach and he grows his crops on beach sand. Yes, beach sand. When Wilson says, "I'm the only farmer out here," you are probably not surprised.[71]

Myrtle Beach, South Carolina, is the renowned seaside town with sixty miles of sandy beach. You probably know that not much grows on beaches, let alone crops. But leave it to Wilson, a third-generation farmer, to figure out how to work with beach soil on his 1,200-acre farm; however, he wouldn't recommend it to anyone. Wilson would tell you that he has learned more from failures than success. Growing crops on good soil is hard enough; now imagine doing it under even tougher circumstances. Beach soil has unique properties, and Wilson needs to understand its composition to increase the chances of a harvest.

The key is knowing your soil—a critical theme in freestyle evangelism. For example, beach sand doesn't support water retention. Knowing and working with this reality, Wilson enhances sandy soil with organic and inorganic material to improve its ability to retain water. Being so close to the ocean, beach sand has high salt content. Too much salt kills plant life. Wilson takes steps to reduce the salt level on his farm.

Farming on beach sand is an art form. Wilson took years of trial and error to figure out beach sand. Over the years, Wilson has learned to apply the blend of fertilizers. Combining the right amount of organic matter, compost, biochar, peat, and others into beach soil is crucial to the success of his harvest. Through his perseverance, Wilson's hard work developing the beach landscape on his farm has yielded soybeans, corn, wheat and other valuable crops.

It is hard to look at this evidence of the importance of soil and not marvel at the success of moon soil and beach sand in producing plant life. Here were situations where nothing was expected to grow and, yet, they succeeded. That is the hidden potency of soil that, through proper nutrition, seed, and water, managed to overcome what might otherwise have been impossible odds. Similarly, no soil is immune from combustion and bearing fruit, no matter how difficult it seems.

Action in the Soil

In the Parable of the Soils (Matthew 13:1–23, Mark 4:1–20, Luke 8:4–15), Jesus uses soil as an analogy to describe the state of people's hearts and minds. The seed, or the word of God, lands on different kinds of soils, and the soil conditions directly impact how the seed grows or doesn't grow. Seeds can grow in different kinds of soil, including harsh environments like moon soil and beach sand or in places with the smallest soil such as tiny pavement or driveway cracks.

When we say that seeds can grow on nearly every surface, what we are really saying is that the soil plays a much bigger role in evangelism than we actually realize. This is because, when we think of evangelism, we think of Billy Graham, Aimee Semple McPherson, George Whitefield, and other charismatic speakers who come to mind. We tend to equate evangelism with sowers of the seed. In other words, the focus of evangelism is on the "doers" of evangelism. If we think of evangelism as the job primarily done by the "doers" or sowers of seed, then what are the people? People are passive "receivers" of the work of sowers.

Our current evangelism doesn't activate everyday Christians because our models rely fundamentally on the "doers" of ministry. Freestyle is the opposite. It puts the focus on the soil or the "receivers." The soil, after all, is where holy combustions happen—not in the hands of the sower. In freestyle, the soil is not passive but a creative participant in evangelism. Not only is the soil where combustions happen but the soil feeds and nurtures the seedling from the moment of germination to its maturation. The seedling is dependent on the soil.

The seed and soil become interlocked in many ways and create something new and unique. When the conditions are met, the seed interacts with the soil, the combustible energy within the seed is released. The seed erupts and starts to grow roots in the soil and will feed on the particular nutrients in the soil. However, soils are uniquely different depending on where they come from. Soil from the arid regions of Arizona will differ from those in the Kansas High Plains or the Green Mountains of Vermont.

The Dust Bowl

During the Dust Bowl, a period of US history that spanned nearly the entire decade of the 1930s, dark clouds of dust storms ravaged the country from the Great Plains to the East Coast. On April 14, 1935, "Black Sunday," as it was later called, was the worst day of the Dust Bowl and the scene on that day could have easily been mistaken for a clip from a Hollywood postapocalyptic movie. The amount of soil that moved on "Black Sunday" was more than 300,000 tons. To put it into perspective, that was twice as much excavated dirt dug out of the Panama Canal—which took seven long years to dig. The dust storms came from all over the Great Plains states, such as Oklahoma, Kansas, Missouri, Nebraska, Texas, and Colorado.

The dust storm on Black Sunday was a thousand miles long; 200 miles across; and 2,000 feet high with 65 mile-per-hour winds. To give you a sense of how massive that is, think of the Empire State Building in New York City, which was the tallest building in the world at the time of its completion. Ride the elevator up to the observation deck, atop the Empire State Building. You can see on a clear day as far as Pennsylvania and Massachusetts with the binocular viewers. This dust storm was taller than the Empire State Building by more than 500 feet.

Manhattan Island, end to end, is 13.4 miles long. This dust storm was 1,000 miles long. It was 200 miles across, which is wider than New Jersey. It swallowed up everything in its path. People tried their best to keep the dust out. They sealed their homes tight but dust still managed to enter through the tiniest of cracks, leaving a dust coating on food, skin and furniture. A survivor of the Dust Bowl, wrote, "We live with the dust, eat it, sleep with it, watch it strip us of possessions and the hope of possessions."[72] Clouds of billowing dust would darken the sky, sometimes for days. After the storm passed, residents shoveled accumulated dust in their driveways and sidewalks like snow. As much as three million tons of topsoil was estimated to have carried off the southern Great Plains on Black Sunday alone. Tall dunes of dust surrounded houses and buildings.

The dust storms on Black Sunday traveled 2,000 miles east as far as Philadelphia, Washington, DC, and New York City, coating buildings and ships with inches of dust. Interestingly, after being hit with dust storms so frequently, people began to tell where a particular dust storm came from. How? They knew by the color of the dust. The Great Plains stretched from Texas to Canada, covering more than ten states. If the dust storm was black, they knew it was from Kansas where the soil was rich with organic matter and humus. If the dust was red, it signaled that the soil came from Oklahoma, specifically Western Oklahoma, where it contained a lot of iron. Gray soil meant that it originated from Colorado and New Mexico.

Each distinct region produced different soils. Similarly, people from different regions, cultures, and communities produce their own distinct soil with nutrients particular to that soil. Just as soil has many layers, beginning with topsoil at the top, people have layers of historical memory, cultural sensibilities, and celebrated triumphs as well as losses and infuriating moments etched in their memory that feed into their sense of self-understanding.

The same seed will grow differently in the Appalachian foothills than the marshy areas of the Louisiana bayou or the rainforest regions along the Pacific Northwest. Likewise, the same seed will react differently to the soil in Hong Kong, Rome, Rio, or Mecca. From a freestyle perspective, evangelism is a dynamic process whereby people's cultural ideals, religious belief systems, and personal experiences play a distinctive role in how they interact with the seed.

Think of beach soil as a product of a complex process that formed over time. Like all other soil, the interaction with its environment profoundly shaped beach soil. The repeated weathering of rocks creates beach soil over a long time. Because of its location, beach nourishment is essential to plant development. Minerals and marine plant life release nutrients and chemicals. However, if the beach soil is too close to the ocean, the soil is under constant stress of being potentially washed off into the water.

Paul's Soil

In the New Testament, Paul explains his unique soil. He admits how his turnaround to Christ may seem absurd to people. A few times in his letters, Paul describes how he was the epitome of a devout first-century Jew—a "Hebrew of Hebrews; as to the law, a Pharisee; as to zeal, a persecutor of the church; as to righteousness under the law, blameless" (Philippians 3:5–6).

Paul was a devout Pharisee who terrorized Christians. He scoured the landscape with self-righteous zeal. In his fanaticism, Paul received letters of authorization from the high priest to seize and arrest Christians in Damascus so that he "might bring them bound to Jerusalem" (Acts 9:2). On the road to Damascus, Paul encountered Jesus and the history of Christianity was forever changed. Paul said, "For I am the least of the apostles, unfit to be called an apostle, because I persecuted the church of God" (1 Corinthians 15:9).

After his holy combustion, Paul began preaching Christ, declaring that "He is the Son of God" (Acts 9:20). Because Paul was one of the finest minds of his day, being trained by Gamaliel, he easily debated and defeated any opposition.[73] Paul "became increasingly more powerful and confounded the Jews who lived in Damascus by proving that Jesus was the Messiah" (v. 22). People were obviously astonished. They wondered, "Is not this the man who made havoc in Jerusalem among those who invoked this name? And has he not come here for the purpose of bringing them bound before the chief priests?" (v. 21).

When Paul made his way to Jerusalem, his reputation as a zealot against everything Christian preceded him. The Christian community heard rumors of his conversion but they thought it was a ruse, a trick to flush them out in order to capture them. They were so intimidated by Paul's ruthless reputation that they refused to meet and receive him. When Paul returned to Jerusalem, "he attempted to join the disciples; and they were all afraid of him, for they did not believe that he was a disciple" (Acts 9:26). It was only after Barnabas brought Paul to the disciples that Paul was able to finally meet them. But Paul wasn't done. "So [Paul] went in and out among them in Jerusalem, speaking boldly in the name of the Lord. He spoke and argued with the Hellenists; but they were attempting to kill him" (vv. 28–29).

"Oh My Gourd!"

"Oh My Gourd" was the headline of a newspaper article.[74] The article reported on the 2021 North Carolina State Fair and the winner of the giant pumpkin category. Twenty-one ginormous pumpkins entered the competition. Each was weighed on a massive scale to the delight of the crowd. The winning pumpkin weighed nearly a ton at 1,965.5 pounds, marking a new record in the annals of North Carolina State Fair history.

You would think that Chris Rodebaugh, the grower of the prize-winning pumpkin, was a farmer or an expert in agricultural sciences. Not quite. Rodebaugh is a dentist. Not only did he start growing pumpkins just three years earlier, but Rodebaugh also had no prior background in farming. His inspiration came during the 2018 West Virginia State Fair where he saw how the pumpkin competition thrilled the crowds. People's faces lit up with delight when they witnessed the weighing of the pumpkins. Rodebaugh adds, "It's just amazement and wonder and it makes everyone child-like."[75] When Rodebaugh decided to start growing giant pumpkins, he picked the most suitable place for the project: the backyard of his single-family house in the suburbs of Lewisburg, West Virginia. He proceeded to plow his backyard which had never had a garden and transformed it into a pumpkin patch.

Once the pumpkin was ready, transporting what was the size of a small car to a trailer and hauling it across state lines to Raleigh was no small task. Once he reached the State Fair, a construction crane was needed to lift and move the massive pumpkin. It was difficult to tell if Rodebaugh would win since many other humongous pumpkins were fighting for the title. The tension was building. "Which pumpkin would win?" people wondered. Rodebaugh observed "the excitement of the crowd."[76] Each pumpkin was weighed in front of the crowd, which determined Rodebaugh's pumpkin as the winner.

How did a full-time dentist manage to grow prize-winning pumpkins as a hobby? This is the question that Rodebaugh gets a lot. He always has the same answer: "know your soil."[77] In the beginning, Rodebaugh was as surprised as anyone how well his pumpkins grew. At the same time, he shouldn't be all that surprised. He carefully studied soil, its chemical components and levels, ideal fertilization, and maintenance. Because the soil was ready, the pumpkin seed experienced a tremendous combustion and produced an amazing fruit. Most of us would look at Chris Rodebaugh's property as nothing more than an ordinary suburban backyard but he saw his soil differently, as capable of producing prize-winning pumpkins. Likewise, if we focus more on the soil, we too can experience unexpected results.

Seed Grows from the Soil

Freestyle evangelism recognizes the subsurface impact that seeds have on soils—a process that I call "turning over the earth."[78] Something happens to the soil when a seed germinates. The gospel seed begins to take hold in the soil. Roots grow from the gospel seed and anchor themselves in the soil where they draw nutrients. As the roots of the gospel grow in the heart and mind, they apply pressure within the soil. The growing roots physically push and break apart soil particles. In many ways, roots are designed to break apart the hardness of soil. Tiny hairs on the root tips loosen the soil by finding and creating space. The breaking apart of soil creates passages for water and air to travel further into the soil to the deeper root zones. The end result is the expansion of the soil structure and overall betterment of the soil as soil aeration and drainage are improved. The expansion of the soil creates air pockets that enable more oxygen to flow.

The "turning over the earth" principle says that a similar breakdown happens in people's minds and hearts as life from the gospel seed begins to take root in a person's heart. The practice of freestyle evangelism acknowledges that the gospel seed—by itself, without any help from humans—can loosen up a person's hardened heart and create a powerful combustion. The gospel seed is more than capable of doing most of the heavy lifting in freestyle evangelism. Freestyle is the "letting go" approach to evangelism whereby we rely on the Holy Spirit to break hardened soil in the individual, rather than humans feeling the burden to "make something happen" in evangelism.

Like roots in the soil, the power of the gospel seed becomes embedded in the person, changing and transforming the person from the inside out. In freestyle evangelism, the burden of the Christianizing process falls to the Holy Spirit who awakens the soul to "Christ in me" consciousness. However, not every converted soul will look the same because each brings their individual inner conflicts, worldviews, and idealized concepts, that is, soil, to their faith formation. In other words, the soil plays a pivotal role in all this.

Uniqueness of Soils

As a living organism, soil is susceptible to strong winds, erosion, surface runoffs, detachment, shrinkage and swelling, loss from denitrification, damage from disease, and so on. In other words, soil is very much like us: prone to the vicissitudes of life.

There are working farmlands in England today that have been farmed since the Middle Ages. One of the oldest is Blackmore Farm about 160 miles west of London. Blackmore has been farmed continuously since the eleventh century and possibly even earlier. We know this from the *Doomsday Book*, a survey of England's landowners and tenants commissioned by William the Conqueror, shortly after claiming the throne at the Battle of Hastings (1066). All of the "owners and occupiers" of Blackmore Farm are listed in the *Doomsday Book* from before 1066 through the present.

In other words, the soil at Blackmore Farm has been worked on for nearly a thousand years. Generation after generation, those on Blackmore have left their imprint on the soil. The current caretakers at Blackmore have to deal with—for better or worse—what how well previous generations have tended to the soil.

Similarly, the soil of America's younger generation is different from the soil of the baby boomers. While this may seem obvious, the idea that evangelism should speak to what people aspire to, dream about, or struggle with is not common. The best way to know your soil is to investigate cultural norms, deeply held values, and particular religious beliefs that are characteristic of a group of people.

Culture is in a constant state of flux and, most of the time, we cannot predict what issue or struggle lies ahead or how they may impact lives. Its environment influences the soil's internal parts and, as a result, people's response to religion changes. For example, the recent changes in Americans' attitude toward religion surprised researchers. In the 2023 *Wall Street Journal* survey, the ways Americans view religion from thirty years ago today are "so dramatic," according to a researcher. The changing view of religion "paints a new and surprising portrait of a changing America."[79]

A part of the reason why *The Wall Street Journal* was so surprised is that they have been surveying Americans for years about values they deemed "very important." In 1998, 62 percent of Americans said religion was very important. In 2019, 48 percent said religion was very important. In 2023, 39 percent said religion was very important. The generational differences could not have been more stark. 55 percent of those aged sixty-five and over said religion was very important but 31 percent of those aged eighteen to twenty-nine said religion was very important, "which was the lowest percentage of all adult age groups."

The poll also revealed a divided country that is becoming more polarized. "Back in the day," one respondent said, members of opposing parties "had a sense of deference to one another," but not anymore. Today, they act like those "in a schoolyard trying to be vengeful and reactive."[80] In fact, the values that *The Wall Street Journal* tested, such as patriotism, having children, and community involvement, have all declined in importance, except one: money. In the past quarter-century, money was mentioned as very important by 43% in the new poll, "up from 31% in 1998."[81]

In many ways, Christianity is an institution and, by extension, evangelism serves institutional goals. While people continue to view Christianity as an institution, the decoupling has already begun, at least in the minds of the younger generation as they are leaving the institutionalized version of Christianity that the previous generations have supported and upheld. They are seeking alternatives, but the church, which is embedded in institutional thinking and culture, has difficulty engaging with new realities.

However, recent destabilizing developments in society have accelerated young people's openness to God. A twenty-six-year-old who previously questioned her belief as a teen, now chooses to believe. She says, "If I ever started to doubt, or believe there wasn't a God, it would send me into a spiral of 'What ifs,' things that I would rather not get into."[82] The hardships endured during the pandemic and social and political unrest have spurred greater interest in spiritual matters and to larger faith-related questions. "In many ways, it [COVID] aged young Americans and they are now turning to the same comfort previous generations have turned to during tragedies for healing and comfort."[83]

An associate dean at Princeton Theological Seminary says, "We are seeing an openness to transcendence among young people that we haven't seen for some time."[84] Their openness to God is particularly surprising given that this younger generation didn't grow up with traditional religion and belief in the transcendence; they "don't associate God with a specific organized religion."[85] Among the eighteen-to-twenty-five-year-olds surveyed in 2023, about one-third say they believe (more than doubt) in the existence of a higher power.[86] How does the church appeal to people who no longer trust them? If our evangelism is indifferent to what people are going through, we miss opportunities to speak to them at crucial moments.

Understand the Soil's Characteristics

At an evangelism conference, I led a discussion about the importance of understanding soil as a critical part of freestyle evangelism. I asked: "What do you think are the highest ideals of today's culture?" In other words, what is their highest priority? What do they want more than anything else? Here are some of their answers:

- "Really, really rich. Lots of wealth."
- "Famous. Justin Bieber famous. Kardashian famous."
- "Have a big impact. Make the world a better place."
- "Live comfortably."
- "No struggle. Peaceful."
- "Try to appear that you have no struggle. Life is easy."

- "No weakness. Struggle equals weakness."
- "Figuring out who you are. Being happy."
- "The 'look' or appearance. Latest trend."
- "People don't want to see others sad. It makes you feel sad."

In a snapshot, here is a list that captures what we are all about. Just about every answer is about the self—or, to be more specific, self-fulfillment, self-advancement, or self-promotion. As I mentioned in the introduction, freestyle appeals to the postmodern mind because the starting point is the individual and how Jesus meets the individual's desires.

The individual's deepest aspirations, frustrations, and longings are the nutrients in the soil. Underneath the surface, the gospel seed interacts with the soil of a person's heart and mind and absorbs the nutrients. The sprouting seed changes the soil and brings new life. For example, when the Samaritan woman encountered Jesus and experienced a holy combustion, she went on an evangelistic crusade to her hometown. It is unsurprising that the first thing she says, before declaring that he is the Messiah, is, "Come and see a man who told me everything I have ever done!" (John 4:29). For the Samaritan woman, her personal grief over failed relationships was bottled up inside. Jesus spoke directly to her pent-up frustrations and released them. What had been the source of her greatest sorrow and pain now became the lead to her evangelistic message.

The first thing that Zacchaeus said, after his holy combustion, was, "Look, half of my possessions, Lord, I will give to the poor; and if I have defrauded anyone of anything, I will pay back four times as much" (Luke 19:8). Both Zacchaeus and the Samaritan woman experienced holy combustions but what made them combustible derived from different nutrients. Zacchaeus's reaction to his combustion shows that his relationship with money was a driving factor in his life. Before meeting Jesus, Zacchaeus may have thought that money would bring him ultimate happiness and became obsessive about gaining more and more wealth but ended up leaving him more disillusioned.

In a loving and nonjudgmental way, Jesus addresses the specific areas of people. Jesus spoke of redemption but the message was unique to Zacchaeus and the Samaritan woman. Freestyle activates people to speak to them where they are, in their particular season and location in life. When we see people for who they really are, we can see how Jesus can meet their specific conditions. Instead of a prepackaged evangelism that is made for a whole group of people, Jesus addressed people individually. He knew their hot buttons, debilitating anxieties, passionate pursuits, and highest concerns in life.

Freestyle shifts the focus of evangelism to the soil, that is, people. If we think evangelism is about strategies and practices, we can easily lose sight of the composition of the soil on which we intend to sow seeds. More than ever in US history (and perhaps human history), society is fractured into countless subcultures and tribes, egged on by social media and the digital revolution. Therefore, the effort to create evangelism programs is very difficult considering the ever-shifting cultural landscape that we live in. Instead of evangelism as a "one-size-fits-all" shirt to cover everyone, freestyle offers a way for individuals to design and create a tailor-made suit just for them. However, in order to relate to people's particular characteristics, we need to investigate the spark points or what ignites the unique nutrients in the soil, which will be the focus of the next chapter.

CHAPTER FIVE

Spark Points

Not long ago, Varun Soni at the University of Southern California (USC) noticed a change among students in the late 2010s. As the Dean of Religious Life, Soni is particularly interested in the spiritual well-being of the campus community and actively listens to their needs. When Soni began his role in 2008, he heard questions from students, as you may expect, about how to live their best lives. They wrestled to find meaning and purpose. They are at a point in their lives, a period of transitioning to adulthood. They are taking steps to make serious decisions on their own and they wanted to know the particular values and life paths that would bring them fulfillment.

However, over the past decade, he observed a shift in the kind of questions that students were asking, a "devastating" development according to Soni.[87] No longer were students asking or interested in the "How should I live?" question. To Soni's surprise, students asked, "*Why* should I live?" Soni could not have predicted that young people who are starting their life in college would struggle with questions about death that leave them distressed and overwhelmed.

To the older generations, it can be difficult to understand what Gen Z is going through. In an article, a blogger explains the debilitating existential questions he and his generation are enduring. He thinks about his reality "obsessively," wondering if his life is a "one big simulation" or if we are here "by the fateful luck of evolution."[88] The obsession with reality spills over to thoughts about death and life after death. He wonders about the meaninglessness of it all and "what a potential insignificant life would mean to me." The constant unabating rehashing of these thoughts has filled him "with dread."

Taking prescribed medication has helped, he admits. However, "so frequent were these thoughts" that they don't quite silence his "fears about existentialism." In other words, the existential questions are his biggest spark points. He says, "I was genuinely concerned about the answers to my existential questions." He continuously wrestles with these questions, "exploring and forging beliefs around my existence, and what life means to me." But in the end, Gibson wonders about the futility of it all. He asks, "How can we make sense of a life that doesn't necessarily make any sense?"

At first, when "Why should I live" questions began to emerge in the student body, Soni was unsure where they were coming from. Perhaps it was an aberration, something unique to his region. After researching the phenomenon and conferring with chaplains across the country, he found it was happening nationwide. "Every year, it seems," Soni says, "I encounter more stress, anxiety, and depression, and more students in crisis on campus."[89] The students coming to campus are "digital natives," meaning they've been watching shows on smartphones and iPads as early as they can remember. Early on, they had social media accounts and can tell you the latest online pop cultural trends but there is a cost. More time and attention to digital media meant less time on interpersonal relationships.

College chaplains have witnessed the developments happening on campuses across the country. College officials are scrambling to hire enough mental health counselors to meet the demand. As the Center for Collegiate Mental Health warned, the number of students turning to mental health services has greatly surpassed the increase in student enrollment. According to the Center, counseling center utilization between 2009 and 2015 "increased by an average of 30–40%, while enrollment increased by only 5%."[90] The report added that increasing demand "is primarily characterized by a growing frequency of students with a lifetime prevalence of threat-to-self indicators."[91] The 2021 Report from the annual Healthy Minds Study, which surveyed 133 college campuses and over ninety-six thousand American college students reflected the same upward trend of students reporting depression and anxiety disorders. The Study highlighted that the number of students seriously contemplating suicide in the past year of its study was "the highest recorded rates in the history of the 15-year-old survey."[92]

Spark Points in People

The "Why should I live" question is an example of a spark point in freestyle evangelism. *Spark point* is a term I use to refer to compressed (and sometimes unresolved) tension nesting in people. Everyone has interests of various kinds but spark points are those that are supremely affecting. For example, the "Why should I live" question, for those who are consumed by it, is a matter that gnaws at them. It doesn't stop. It thirsts for a resolution.

Spark points don't have to be dramatic. The spark point for the woman in the Parable of the Lost Coin (Luke 15:8–10) was the anguish after losing one of her ten silver coins. This spark point was so intense that her single life focus—at that season in her life—was to seek and find this coin. Everything else in her life became secondary. She carefully inspects every square inch of her house. When she finds the coin, she has a combustion and is overjoyed beyond imagination. "When she has found it, she calls together her friends and neighbors, saying, 'Rejoice with me, for I have found the coin that I had lost'" (v. 9).

In another parable with a similar theme, Jesus says, "The kingdom of heaven is like treasure hidden in a field, which someone found and hid; then in his joy he goes and sells all that he has and buys that field" (Matthew 13:44). In the following parable, Jesus says, "Again, the kingdom of heaven is like a merchant in search of fine pearls; on finding one pearl of great value, he went and sold all that he had and bought it" (Matthew 13:45–46). The "treasure" or "pearl" is the spark point for the individual, and discovering it stimulates a tremendous response that leads to a powerful reaction. Today, in our practice of evangelism, we sometimes disregard the fact that the woman is desperately searching for her lost coin and the man for pearls and, instead, present them with something other than what they are thirsting for.

Freestyle recognizes that the "lost coin," "treasure," and "pearl" carry great significance for individuals, as they symbolize what is the most pressing and valuable for the individual. As Jesus says, "For where your treasure is, there your heart will be also" (Matthew 6:21). In the Parable of the Lost Coin, it is *her* lost coin, a special coin that she holds in the highest esteem. When someone finds a "treasure" in a field, we don't know what the treasure is, but, to *that* individual, it is priceless. A merchant discovers a pearl so valuable that "he went and sold all that he had." Like the Samaritan woman who is thirsting for "living water," freestyle evangelism is knowing what they are thirsting after and delivering Jesus to them in a way that speaks to their thirst.

Spark points are infused with potent energy to move individuals when ignited. For example, if those with the nagging question, "Why should I live," were to discover the "treasure" that satisfied their desperate search, they would be aroused into great jubilation and action. What makes a spark point so potent is the unmistakable way it organically spurs people into action. Spark points evoke strong emotional reactions, such as in those who found the coin, treasure, and pearl. Addressing someone's spark point speaks to the deepest core of who they are. On a larger scale, a spark point can be felt across a community, subculture, or nation, such as when a country experiences a shutdown from a viral epidemic, the triumph of winning the World Cup or the craze from a pop-culture phenomenon.

A spark point may appear from nowhere, caused by an unexpected development or sudden loss. A spark point can also be very personal to an individual. In the Parable of the Prodigal Son, the younger brother passionately pursued life but mistakenly presumed it wasn't with his father but in worldly pleasure. He went full throttle for wild living and eventually found himself broke and abandoned. His spark point was the dissonance that produced an internal conflict, a disillusionment between his desire for what he thought was life's fulfillment and the harsh reality of his disappointment. Individual spark points don't need to be as dramatic as the younger brother's but they are deeply affecting, like a restless undercurrent swirling under the surface.

Spark points are gateways. They can be emotional connectors, such as traditions, strong beliefs, or idealized goals. Some spark points are deeply interwoven in a person's soul and remain as a latent impulse. These spark points are in the soil and when gospel seeds interact with the combustible elements of the soil, a holy combustion erupts. What makes spark points so important in freestyle evangelism? Igniting an individual's spark point unleashes the wellspring of the "living water" within a person. Nagging questions and themes can intensify like a pressure cooker. Holy combustion is the release of the trapped steam. For many Gen Zers, the existential questions are the most potent, meaningful, and piercing questions they have. How can the church respond in a way that speaks to their spark points?

Paul's Message at Areopagus

For ancient Greeks, Areopagus had deep religious significance. Areopagus (or "Hill of Ares") was named for Ares, the god of war, who, in Greek mythology, was on trial at Areopagus, and later acquitted for the murder of Poseidon's son. Orestes, another figure in Greek mythology, was on the lam for murder. The Furies, goddesses of justice and revenge, relentlessly pursued and then captured Orestes, who was put on trial at Areopagus and was later pardoned by Athena, the patron goddess of Athens.

In the New Testament, Areopagus was the epicenter of the brightest minds in the Greek world, and it was also the Supreme Council of the Athenian government. Philosophers, politicians, and nobles assembled at Areopagus to debate the universe and their place in it. "All the Athenians and the foreigners living there," according to Acts 17:21, "would spend their time in nothing but telling or hearing something new."

Only the most esteemed orators and minds were invited to speak at the Areopagus, so how did Paul get himself invited? In the marketplace, Paul "argued" and "debated" with Epicurean and Stoic philosophers, that is, professional philosophers who were masters of rhetoric (vv. 17–18). Paul proved himself more than capable of holding a debate with them. Then the philosophers invited Paul to the Areopagus, "May we know what this new teaching is that you are presenting? It sounds rather strange to us, so we would like to know what it means" (vv. 19–20).

When Paul addresses the distinguished crowd at Areopagus, what would he say? How would he relate the gospel to an audience deeply soaked in Greek paganism? As we shall see, Paul communicated the gospel by speaking to, perhaps, one of their biggest spark points: the enthusiastic worship of their gods. The ancient Greek calendar was filled with festivals for their gods, some lasting weeks. Cities, towns, and mountains, such as Mount Olympus where the twelve major gods led by Zeus dwelled, had a patron god or gods. In Galatians 4:9–11, Paul rebukes Galatian Christians for turning away from the one, true God for "the weak and beggarly elemental spirits" (v. 9). Paul learned that they had returned to worshipping demonic gods, "You are observing special days, and months, and seasons, and years" (v. 10). At this point, Paul is exasperated. "How can you want to be enslaved to them again?" he asks. "I am afraid that my work for you may have been wasted" (v. 11).

At Areopagus, Paul gets up to speak: "Athenians, I see how extremely religious are in every way" (Acts 17:22). High religious observance, marked by festivals, games, sacrifices, and celebrations, was imprinted on the Greeks' minds. Athens was "full of (religious) idols" (v. 16), representing many of the major gods in the Greek pantheon. However, with countless gods around, it was impossible to know and worship every one of them, so the Greeks found a way to include them. Paul says, "For as I went through the city and looked carefully at the objects of your worship, I found among them an altar with the inscription, 'To an unknown God'" (Acts 17:23). The reason for this is quite simple. To avoid giving offense to unknown gods that they didn't know about, they had an idol made for them.

The possibility of giving offense to the gods stoked great fear among the Greeks. And Paul zeroed in on this fear. Greek gods were spiteful and went on a vengeful warpath against each other or humans when offended. The Greek religious system depended on enthusiastic participation to celebrate and appease the gods. Why? Humans are susceptible to their wrath and punishment if the gods are not appeased through their prayers, sacrifices, and festivals. Paul opened their hearts to hearing and receiving the gospel seed by pinpointing what every Greek feared.

Paul says, "What therefore you worship as unknown, this I proclaim to you" (v. 23). He proceeds to say:

> (24) The God who made the world and everything in it, he who is Lord of heaven and earth, does not live in shrines made by human hands, (25) nor is he served by human hands, as though he needed anything, since he himself gives to all mortal life and breath and all things. (26) From one ancestor he made all nations to inhabit the whole earth, and he allotted the times of their existence and the boundaries of the places where they would live, (27) so that they would search for God and perhaps grope for him and find him—though indeed he is not far from each one of us. (28) For "in him we live and move and have our being"; as even

some of your own poets have said, "For we too are his offspring." (29) Since we are God's offspring, we ought not to think that the deity is like gold, or silver, or stone, an image formed by the art and imagination of mortals. (30) While God has overlooked the times of human ignorance, now he commands all people everywhere to repent, (31) because he has fixed a day on which he will have the world judged in righteousness by a man whom he has appointed, and of this he has given assurance to all by raising him from the dead.

For Paul to speak to their spark point, he needed to understand the mind and heart of the Greek, what they truly cared about, and what their belief systems were. Paul managed to connect the gospel in a way that connected his listeners to the most meaningful thing. Paul didn't condescend their religious beliefs and practices, even though they were antithetical to what he believed. Instead, he acknowledged them and spoke to their nagging questions and greatest fears.

Denzel Washington: "It's Culture"

In 2016, the cast of the movie *Fences* sat for a promotional interview with Urban View, a channel that discusses Black culture, voices, and politics. A four-time Oscar-nominated film, *Fences* is about a working-class African American family in Pittsburgh in the 1950s. Troy Maxson, the father of the family, is a middle-aged man who works as a garbage collector. The film reveals Maxson, played by Denzel Washington, who also produced and directed *Fences*, struggling with his own personal demons, lost dreams, and troubled relationships with his family, particularly his son. His wife, Rose, played by Viola Davis, navigates the fraught relationships.

The interviewer asked the cast about August Wilson, the late playwright who wrote *Fences*. Before he approved the on-screen adaptation, Wilson insisted that a Black director guide the movie. The interviewer asked, "So, why did [Wilson] need a Black director? Could a white director not have made it work?"[93] It's an interesting point. Couldn't a Latino or Asian person direct *Fences* and make it work? The answer is obviously yes. There are many prize-winning Latino and Asian directors who would have been terrific. The same goes for churches as well. Could a Latino or Asian person pastor a Black church? And vice versa? Absolutely. So, what do race and ethnicity have to do with directing a movie about an African American family and community? Could a person of any background do as good of a job in directing "Fences"?

Denzel Washington answers, "It's not color. It's culture."[94]

"Explain the difference," the interviewer asks.

Washington says, "Steven Spielberg did *Schindler's List*. Martin Scorsese did *Goodfellas*, right? Steven Spielberg could direct *Goodfellas*. Martin Scorsese probably could have done a good job with *Schindler's List*. But there are cultural differences." As Washington points out, Spielberg and Scorsese would have done a fine job with each other's films (if given the opportunity), but there are cultural nuances that the legendary directors are not privy to. To illustrate his point, Washington looks at the interviewer and the audience and says,

> I know, you know, we all know [in the African American community] what it is when a hot comb hits your head on a Sunday morning, what it smells like. That's a cultural difference, not just color difference. So, it's the culture.

Washington is referring to the method used by African American women to straighten hair, especially on Sunday mornings before church. Although many use electric hot combs, many still prefer the old-fashioned method of heating it really hot over a stove. The process of heating up a hot comb and using it on your hair is cultural insight. It produces a distinct sound and smell, which Washington was referring to.

The interviewer then turns to Viola Davis and asks, "You know about a hot comb scenario?"

Before Davis has a chance to answer, Washington jumps in and says, "She knows nothing about a hot comb."

The live audience erupts in laughter. Looking at Davis, Denzel Washington adds, "You don't know nothing about..."—then Washington makes a "hiss" sound while gesturing with his finger touching his microphone. Davis breaks out in laughter. The whole cast and audience join in the funny moment. Then Washington says, "See how everybody laughs. That's a cultural difference. That's not a race difference."

The "hot comb scenario" is an example of cultural insight. When people have cultural insight into a particular subculture or community, they have inside knowledge of their deepest values and worldview. For those who don't know what the "hot comb scenario" is, they would have missed the humor completely. Spark points are often embedded in cultural knowledge. And our aspirations and dreams are often intertwined in our many cultural and subcultural formations.

Cultural Bonds

If you were given a "friendship quilt," how would you react? Would you value a "friendship quilt"? To those in Pennsylvania Dutch culture, receiving a "friendship quilt" was an emotional experience, moving many to tears.

Although it is practiced less today, "friendship quilts" in the past were given with much affection to those who were moving away. Groups of women would come together with squares made by each woman with her name stitched on them. Then they would embroider the squares together to form a quilt. A colorful quilt made of different contributed squares from loved ones becomes a testimonial of love. There were instances where students made a "friendship quilt" for their beloved teacher who was about to move to another state.

The spark point for the Bee Party, mentioned in chapter 3, was the likeminded passion for beekeeping. As participants in the party discovered, they were part of the same subculture and of one mind regarding the special role of bees. They showed up and discovered others who cared for bees just as much as they did. Pastor Lee and Mills witnessed sparks flying once it became clear that the group had the same concerns for bees and nature. As they discussed how bees are absolutely essential for pollinating our fruits and gardens, they found kindred spirits.

It was as if the proverbial light bulb went off when conversations took off. Their deeply held values were acknowledged and genuinely appreciated. "You care for bees and they take care of you," one person said. They loved how bees reward you with honey when you take care of them. They picked each other's brains for maintenance tips. They shared their knowledge about how bees talk to each other in a kind of a bee language. They loved how they could share that love and passion with others who thought just like them. The fact that the Bee Party went so well surprised everyone. They enjoyed themselves so much that they wanted to know when the next party was happening. Best of all, the Bee Party was mobilized very quickly with no financial cost to the church.

Understanding Millennials and Gen Z

At the evangelism conference, I split the room into small groups. I wanted them to consider what's really important to those in the thirty-and-under age group. After some discussion, we got back together and we shared some of their answers. Below are some of the feedback:

- Nonjudgmental / open-minded to new ideas.
- Asking about anyone's interest.

- Experience over things, possessions.
- Antagonist to the future, feeling doom.
- Diversity except generational diversity.
- Instant connection via social media.
- Incredible drive to community.
- Quick advancement over loyalty with expectation that.
- they'll have multiple careers.
- Very socially proactive / active mindset.
- Find a place to be active.
- Find uniqueness over something already established.
- Pragmatic and realistic / look for balance.
- Overall perception matters—how they're perceived by peers and older generation.
- Environmental concerns.
- Burden of issues handed down from prior generation that they want to address.
- Thirty is old.
- Talking about their drama, loss.
- Talking about their baggage—less taboo now.
- Expectation of scarcity.
- Cheerful nihilism / great resignation.
- Anxiety and mental health, fragility.
- "I just can't deal with the world today."
- Taking a mental sabbath.
- Shame that you haven't done enough.

Spark Points

- Embody the shame.

How do these comments help us with evangelism with those thirty and under? First, they offer a way of making sense of the younger generations. They provide us with direction for how to see their mindset and values, which are quite different from those of the older generations. For example, I never heard of "taking a mental sabbath" when I was growing up but, for millennials and Gen Zers, active maintenance of mental health is a high priority. Their perspective is not surprising when you consider what they are going through. According to the 2022 Annual Report from the Center for Collegiate Mental Health, mental health issues loom large for the younger generation. For example, the report discovered that social anxiety exceeded general anxiety "with the largest 12-year increase."[95] Also in the report, the history of trauma exceeded previous counseling as the mental health history item "with the largest 10-year increase."[96] A 2022 study by McKinsey revealed similar results. They found Gen Zers with "least positive life outlook, including lower levels of emotional and social well-being than older generations."[97]

"Their internal calculus is different [from other generations]," says a staffer at a college campus ministry.[98] He is referring to the unique mindset of Gen Z. To older generations, they are hard to read. In fact, they at times may seem noncommittal or, worse, rude. If you for example invite them out for coffee, you may get a text like: "I'd love to get coffee with you as long as I don't have something else" or "I'll meet you there unless something changes." They don't mean to offend anyone by their lack of committing; they are simply "just anxious."[99]

If we include spark points in our consideration of evangelism, we reframe the way we think about evangelism because spark points offer a way of making sense of the people we are trying to reach—as opposed to presenting something premade for them without regard to what they want or need. They provide us with direction for how to go about igniting a holy combustion. The balance of this book will take these ideas of holy combustions and spark points and apply them to situations and consider the possible outcomes and consequences. What happens when we speak to spark points and ignite combustions? The answers may surprise you.

CHAPTER SIX

Speak to Spark Points

Pastor Nancy Walton shared a story about a tragic loss that impacted her neighborhood in our evangelism follow-up meeting. Her church is in a neighborhood known for brewpubs, hippies/hipsters, and counterculture vibes. Christmas was fast approaching and she was considering whether or not to have a Blue Christmas service.

If you're not familiar with a Blue Christmas service, it is a church service that creates a sacred space to allow for people to acknowledge struggles and loss of loved ones in a season of celebration. A Blue Christmas service takes a somber, yet, hopeful tone. Lights are lowered while soft music plays in the background. Overall, the darker setting creates a serious mood as well as a sense of privacy to enable individuals to grapple with personal anxieties that can feel overwhelming. They grieve over loss and the service enables them to bring it before God's presence.

In the end, Pastor Walton decided to hold a Blue Christmas service. What tipped her over was the untimely death of a young woman who overdosed and was found dead across the street from the church. Although her city is a tourist destination, the people in her community are uniquely attuned to social justice issues and the plight of those trying to sort out their lives. Even though the young woman was homeless and dealing with substance abuse, they embraced her and looked after her. Pastor Walton said, "Folks knew her and had a relationship with her. And had seen glimmers of possibilities of new life for her." Her death devastated the community and their grief was palpable. She added, "That shook up the neighborhood, for sure."

Pastor Walton made a bold move that she knew came with risk. She opened the Blue Christmas service to the wider community and invited key members and organizations from the neighborhood to participate in the service, including the anarchists across the street who ran a bookstore. "I never had anarchists as neighbors," she said with a smile. "It's an odd relationship but it's a good one."

She told everyone, "It's a hard time of the year. Let's just be together and acknowledge God." In an open-ended manner, she invited folks "to bring something to share, what holds them together through grief." Everything was going well during the service. People shared touching stories and words of remembrance. It was "beautiful," but something changed in the air at a precise moment—a "stillpoint" to use her words. Everyone felt it. It was as if they were hit with a powerful but calm sense of belonging and healing that left them awestruck. A young woman from the anarchist bookstore brought an instrument Pastor Walton had never seen before. From her description, the instrument seemed to be an Indian harmonium, a small wooden box with keys like a piano and a flap used to manually pump air into the instrument like an accordion.

The young woman needed a moment to set up her instrument atop a table. She began playing the instrument and started singing a song her grandfather taught her. She told the audience she would sing this song whenever she was sad. It was at this point when the service "turned." The moment was a cathartic release of emotions experienced collectively as a group. It's hard to describe what happened but everyone in church felt it and, more importantly, experienced it together. Walton observed, "We all had this collective realization of 'that was what we are here for.'" I asked her to describe the impact a little more. "It was celebratory and a memory," she said. "It brought back these beautiful memories even while it was an acknowledgment that she was sad that she lost her grandfather." The song had the dynamic effect of drawing and uniting people of diverse and divergent backgrounds together in common grief over the loss of loved ones. The bonding was unexpected. The two sides coexisted in the neighborhood, acknowledging each other, but not quite comingling. Through this powerful experience, they saw each other, not as people with different lifestyles or views, but individuals with their own lived experiences. She described the emotional loosening as the "holding of the breath and then a deep release of the breath."

In the following Sunday service, which fell on Christmas Day in 2022, she observed something she did not expect. She was surprised to see some church members who were at the

Blue Christmas service displaying genuine interest in their "unhoused friends" from the neighborhood. On Christmas morning, they sat down next to them for breakfast and were "just chatting it up." She was amazed at how their hearts had changed. The reverberating effects of the holy combustion were felt by everyone. She said, "I think the Spirit kept moving."

What she began to realize was that the Blue Christmas service had a much deeper impact than she first thought—for both sides. I asked her, "How did boundaries and walls between them break down?" She replied, "The desire to have 'us-them' language, all of that has been breaking down." She noticed changes in the attitude of her church members. "It's turned from 'we're serving you' and 'this is what we are able to do' to hearing and learning their story." She said, "We've had better understanding of us all being on not different levels of service or receiving service but that we're all on the same level."

Pastor Nancy Walton would tell you that the sudden turnaround was not scripted or expected. None of the glowing results were planned but her leadership was instrumental in creating the conditions for a holy combustion to ignite. First, she spotted the spark points, those combustible elements that suddenly appeared in her neighborhood. She sensed the undercurrent of tension around her and acted quickly to enable its release within sacred space. Spark points show up unexpectedly and disappear just as quickly but she seized the moment by extending welcome to neighbors who remained "skeptical" about the church and kept an arm's length from them. She saw how they were grieving over the young woman who died. I asked her if she thought that the neighborhood residents felt—as a community—that they let the young woman down. "Definitely," she replied,

> I think there was guilt and remorse, that each of us missed something, like checking up on her. Then, there was the systemic guilt of, "Why didn't we have shelter open early enough? Why isn't our city doing more?"

I asked, "Then, the guilt was compounded with some anger?"

"Sure," she replied.

Second, she enabled those who came to the Blue Christmas service to express themselves in their own way—a risky move that many would not have been able to do, for fear of things going awry and potential adverse reactions from their own members. Before the service, she said, "I heard 'one person may say something from this group,' 'one person may sing a song from this group,' but I didn't know who was doing what." Allowing people to be themselves built trust and helped them to open up. She said, "If I had to try micromanage and say, 'What are you doing?' or 'What's your style?' or 'What's your reading?' or 'Oh, that's not appropriate,' we would have missed that evangelism opportunity."

Spark points are like pressurized chambers. Suppressed energy is released if the pressure valve is opened. The intense emotions, such as those brought about by the death of the young woman, for example, can be widely felt by a neighborhood, region, or country. Spark points are everywhere, and they can suddenly appear without warning. Few of us would imagine grief as a spark point but the collective heartbreak and sadness felt by the community demanded a resolution. The Blue Christmas service spoke to *that* spark point and, as a result, released a powerful sense of healing and unity and opened new unforeseen pathways for people to experience Jesus. Pastor Walton remarked, "All of it felt holy. We didn't have to 'preach Jesus.' There was plenty of Jesus present. That was without having to be an apologist either."

The results were remarkable, but no one expected things would go this well. It took a spark to ignite the combustion and a genuine outflow of goodwill toward each other ensued, something that cannot be manufactured or imitated. Think about it differently. Imagine doing evangelism without a spark. It may feel sluggish like trying to push a dead car that won't start. A tiny spark is all that is needed to start the engine of a semitruck that is powerful enough to move cargo weighing up to eighty thousand pounds. The possibility of holy combustion initiating evangelism to move—on its own— might be the hardest aspect of freestyle evangelism for people to visualize. Freestyle creates the self-generating momentum to keep the engine in motion.

Spark points are embedded in people but they vary according to ethnic groups, subcultures, generations, and life experiences. Speaking to particular spark points requires an awareness of what the people around them are experiencing or have endured in the past—for good or bad. Far from a "one-size-fits-all" approach to evangelism, freestyle aims to address the particular spark points in people. In this chapter, we examine conversations in the New Testament that provide important clues to understanding the relationship between spark points and combustion.

Jesus to Peter: "I Will Make You Fish for People"

Imagine the day Jesus called Peter. Along the shores of the Sea of Galilee, Peter and his brother Andrew were "casting a net into the lake" (Matthew 4:18). They were fishermen, just like their father and, perhaps, his father before him. Fishing was his livelihood, and Peter was good at it, but he wondered what his life would be like if he pursued his dreams. The disquieted sense that he hadn't quite lived his full potential was his spark point and Jesus tapped into it when he said to him, "Follow me, and I will make you fish for people" (Matthew 4:19, Mark 1:17).

When Jesus called Peter, he did not overlook his livelihood as a fisherman; he helped Peter realize his full potential by affirming who he was. When Jesus said, "Fish for people," those words struck a deep chord in Peter's heart. He "immediately" stopped what he was doing and left everything behind to follow Jesus.

Being aware of Peter's personality, Jesus knew challenging him would ignite a fire within him. Fishing is a tough profession. You work long, exhausting hours and you may have nothing to show for a day's work when you return to shore empty-handed. Peter was a man of action, impetuous at times. He could be hotheaded and say things on the spur of the moment but when he acts, it is decisive and full of conviction. When Jesus said, "I will make you fish for people," Peter knew what Jesus was referring to. Fishing for people is just as hard as fishing for fish but Peter is up to the challenge. Jesus knew Peter was a resilient kingdom-builder and, as we later witnessed, that was exactly what Peter became: a consequential leader of the early church. Peter was the name that Jesus gave him, which means "rock" (*petros*) in Greek, as Jesus told him in Matthew 16:18, "You are Peter, and on this rock I will build my church, and the gates of Hades will not prevail against it."

Peter became one of the chief pillars of the New Testament church. More than any other disciple, Peter demonstrated faith in a bold and "outside-the-box" way. As an example, Peter challenged Jesus to let him walk on water, an interaction that will be examined in chapter 9. Christians today remember Peter as a towering figure but he was hardly such a person when Jesus first called him on the shores of the Sea of Galilee. Jesus brought out in Peter a whole new side of him that he had never imagined he was capable of. And it all started with a spark.

Samaritan Woman at the Well

The Samaritan woman who met Jesus at the well was from the city of Sychar in Samaria but she wanted to be far away from the crowd. This was demonstrated by her action of coming to the well at noon in order to avoid contact with anyone. Her reaction to Jesus when asked for a drink, "How is that you, a Jew, ask a drink of me, a woman of Samaria?" (John 4:9) displays a tough exterior that may be a function of a lifetime of criticism. Her response was abrupt and didn't care for this man who interrupted her routine.

How would Jesus speak to someone when they are defiant, even antagonistic? Are there any spark points in this situation? First, Jesus asks for water, then turns the tables around and offers her water, but not just any kind of water. It's "living water" (v. 10). She is not impressed. She may have thought he was joking. She replies, "You have no bucket, and the well is deep." How are you supposed to get it? You cannot "get that living water" (v. 11).

Her barbs at Jesus continue. She says, "Are you greater than our ancestor Jacob, who gave us the well, and with his sons and his flocks drank from it?" (v. 12). The statement that Jacob was "our ancestor" was like a punch in the gut to any Jew since they revere Jacob as "the father of the children of Israel." Jews regarded Samaritans as "half-breed," "unclean," and religious apostates and to listen to a Samaritan woman claiming Jacob as their ancestor was, at the very least, provocative.

She is ready to trade verbal blows with Jesus but he doesn't take the bait and, instead, says something that lowers her temperature and helps her to become open-minded and vulnerable. Jesus tells her he has something she truly wants. Jesus says, "Everyone who drinks of this water will be thirsty again." He continues, "But those who drink of the water that I will give them will never be thirsty. The water that I will give will become in them a spring of water gushing up to eternal life" (v. 13–14).

Her demeanor changes and she asks Jesus for this water. She responds, "Sir, give me this water, so that I may never be thirsty or have to keep coming here to draw water" (v. 15). She still thinks what Jesus is offering is physical water and is delighted at the thought of never coming back to the well. Jesus tells her, "Go, call your husband, and come back."

When we do evangelism in the church, we would never consider engaging people's personal lives, especially their insecurities or vulnerabilities. However, Jesus addressed her greatest disappointment: failed relationships. We can only imagine the look on her face when Jesus asked her to call her husband. At this point, she could have become antagonistic toward Jesus and asked him why he was getting into her personal life. Instead, she looks at Jesus and decides to be real. She admits, "I have no husband." Jesus says, "You are right in saying, 'I have no husband'; for you have had five husbands, and the one you have now is not your husband. What you have said is true!" (John 4:17-18).

Spark points can be a tinderbox of emotions without an outlet for release. In other words, it's pressure sealed—or combustible. With honesty, nonjudgment, and compassion, Jesus addressed the core issues of her life that were her spiritual tipping points. The pressurized contents of her life were released and a tremendous outpouring ensued.

At the same time, however, we know it wasn't easy for her to open up to Jesus. She would have no doubt resisted the urge to lower her guard, especially to a stranger, but, her unwavering belief in God that was lying beneath her tough exterior broke through the surface. Jesus encourages her to be real when he says, "God is spirit, and those who worship him must worship in spirit and truth" (John 4:24). Jesus tells her not to be afraid to come before God just as she is. He inspires her to sincerely approach God with all of her heart with passion and truth.

Jesus says worship of God is not confined to a location like "this mountain nor in Jerusalem" (v. 21). "True worshippers," Jesus says, "will worship the Father in spirit and truth (v. 23)," again repeating the words "in spirit and truth" to emphasize that God wants her to worship with her whole heart, including everything about her, "for the Father seeks such as these to worship him" (John 4:23). Jesus's words had the effect of bridging the distance between her and God and, in addition, redefining her past from a stigma to the flashpoint of her deliverance.

What had been a source of shame now became the launching point for her new evangelistic ministry. Powerful emotions, longings, and passions drive spark points. Her combustion produced so much excitement and joy that she left her water jar right there, ran back to the city, and told everyone, "Come and see a man who told me everything I have ever done!" (John 4:29).

Previously, she ran away from her past but, now, that is the first thing she talks about after her holy combustion. The townspeople no doubt know her personal story and how she had tried so hard to keep it under wraps but now she's running around shouting, "Come and see a man who told me everything I have ever done!" The people in the city were obviously stunned to see her talking so openly about her personal life.

Her testimony was so compelling and authentic that they had to see this Jesus. When people combust, they are, in effect, releasing Jesus to everyone they meet. "They left the city and were on their way to him" (v. 30). In spite of the fact that Jesus is Jewish and of a different religion from Samaritans, they nevertheless came to believe Jesus as the Messiah because of her. "Many Samaritans from that city believed in him because of the woman's testimony, 'He told me everything I have ever done'" (v. 39). What is also amazing is that Jesus restored the Samaritan woman to her community that she had previously tried very hard to avoid. The people said to the woman, "It is no longer because of what you said that we believe, for we have heard for ourselves, and we know that this is truly the Saviour of the world" (v. 42).

It was a wild scene. We can only imagine the dumbfounded look on the faces of Jesus's disciples as they witnessed an entire city erupting in holy combustions. Jesus turns to his disciples and tells them, "Look around you, and see how the fields are ripe for harvesting" (v. 35). Spark points can be found in the unlikeliest of places.

Zacchaeus

Zacchaeus was a high-ranking government official who became a follower of Jesus. Finding his spark point, however, was not as easy as it looked. As the chief tax collector, Zacchaeus supervised tax collection over a region, which meant he managed an army of tax collectors who worked for him. In the Roman Empire, the office of chief tax collector was auctioned to the highest bidder. The winning bidder was obligated to pay Rome the contracted amount but was allowed to keep whatever they collected over the bid. Zacchaeus owned the contract for the district and he in turn hired tax collectors at the local level.

Similarly, these lower-level tax collectors owed a certain amount to Zacchaeus and were allowed to keep anything over that amount. You can see how people viewed tax collectors as corrupt and openly called them "sinners" since it was easy to overcharge people—and they couldn't do anything about it. In the ancient Jewish commentary on the law, tax collectors were classified in the same group as robbers, thieves, and criminals.[100]

Levi was an example of a lower-level tax collector. He was sitting in a tax booth along the lakeside when Jesus said, "Follow me." Levi got up from his tax booth and "followed him" (Mark 2:14). The reason why Levi's tax booth was located by the lakeside port is that he collected customs taxes on those conducting commercial trade such as fishermen exporting dried fish or farmers transporting crops.

With only a handful of tax districts in Judea, Levi would have no doubt heard of Zacchaeus, a chief tax collector. The Bible says Zacchaeus was "rich" (Luke 19:2). Zacchaeus led an affluent life, surrounded by rich and connected friends. Even though he reached the height of prosperity, his gilded existence didn't bring meaning and purpose as he thought.

Then one day, he could hear a commotion in the streets. People were excited. Word was spreading fast in the streets from person to person. There was a buzz in the air. He discovered it was Jesus and he was coming to Jericho! Everyone—including Zacchaeus—stopped what they were doing and rushed to Jericho's main thoroughfare, which Jesus and his disciples would be passing through.

Zacchaeus was so excited but there was a problem. People had already flooded the main road—end to end. Rows and rows of people had already gathered and Zacchaeus, being short, had no way of seeing Jesus over the people. He darted here and there, looking for a spot but to no success. It seemed all hope was lost but Zacchaeus doesn't give up. He sees a sycamore tree and climbs it to get a bird's-eye view. Some people laughed at Zacchaeus, a grown man of his political position up in a tree but he doesn't care. Then, everyone could hear noise from far away. It was Jesus. The noise was getting louder as he approached.

Jesus was at the center and mobs of people orbited around him. As he came closer to the sycamore tree, Jesus saw Zacchaeus. Zacchaeus had never met Jesus before but, somehow, Jesus knew his name. "Zacchaeus!" Jesus shouted.

"Hurry and come down; for I must stay at your house today" (Luke 19:5). An eerie hush descended upon the crowds. When people mentioned the name "Zacchaeus" in public, it was usually in disgust or as a curse. No one ever said anything good when they mentioned his name, but here was Jesus shouting—in front of the entire city—the name of Zacchaeus as if he was he were a good friend he hadn't seen in a while.

Zacchaeus cannot believe it. He excitedly escorts Jesus to his house where he throws the biggest party of his life. Jesus triggers a combustion within Zacchaeus and he could not contain himself. In front of all the witnesses, he stands up and says, "Lord, half of my possessions, Lord, I will give to the poor; and if I have defrauded anyone of anything, I will pay back four times as much" (Luke 19:8).

Onlookers could not believe their ears. Here was a guy who devoted his life to wealth building, but now he's giving it away. No one ever imagined that Zacchaeus would become an evangelist for Jesus. Yet, somehow, that's exactly what happened. Zacchaeus's spark point was ignited and this notorious tax collector began to sing the praises of Jesus to everyone. This surely must have been a sight to behold.

How did Zacchaeus's encounter with Jesus lead to a holy combustion? The Bible doesn't tell us what was said between them but, considering how his combustion led to giving away his wealth, we can surmise that Jesus talked about the meaning of life and the pursuit of money. Perhaps Jesus asked Zacchaeus what all his efforts to find life by becoming rich has gotten him. Did that make him happier? Did money bring him peace and joy or trouble and misery? When Zacchaeus became honest and vulnerable, Jesus offered him true riches and the possibility of God's redemption, even for someone like him.

Jesus: "Who Touched Me?"

The story of the woman who approached Jesus to receive healing from hemorrhages is mentioned in all three synoptic gospels (Matthew 9:20–22; Mark 5:25–34; Luke 8:43–48). Twelve years of her condition have left her penniless. "She had endured much under many physicians, and had spent all that she had; and she was no better, but rather grew worse" (Mark 5:26). If she had it her way, she would have liked to disappear from the scene as if no one knew she was there but Jesus would not let that happen. However, it would have been easy to slip out without detection since she was in a large crowd. She drew closer to Jesus and decided, by faith, to touch Jesus to receive healing.

But how would she go about it? She had options. She could hold his hand, pat his back, or grab his arm. She reached out and touched "the fringe" of his cloak (Matthew 9:20, Luke 8:43). Readers often overlook this small detail. The word *fringe* is translated from "tassels" (*tzitzit* in Hebrew)—the specially knotted ritual fringes of a Jewish prayer cloak or shawl (*tallit* in Hebrew). Observant Jews today still wear prayer shawls and on the four corners are tassels (or "fringes") that remind them of God's commandments.

The white cords of the tassel also represented the purity or sanctity of God's commands. Think of the prayer shawl as a large square-shaped woolen cloth with tassels on each of the four corners. When wearing it, the four corners completely cover the individual, with two tassels in the front and two in the back. When people pray while covered with a prayer shawl, they hold the tassels in their hands, a ritual that the woman knew well.

We do not know but she could have prayed earnestly for her healing while holding a tassel of the prayer shawl that Jesus was wearing. Walking alongside Jesus and holding a tassel, she could have made her heartfelt request to God. Jesus immediately sensed it: His healing power was released. Jesus stopped in his tracks. He turned around and faced the crowd and asked, "Who touched me?" (Luke 8:45).

His disciples were baffled. People surrounded Jesus and they were rubbing shoulder to shoulder against him. Peter pointed out the obvious, "Master, the crowds surround you and press in on you" (Luke 8:45). Jesus was undeterred. He waited for her to speak up. People looked at each other puzzled and "all denied it" (Luke 8:46). Jesus just stood there, waiting. Once the woman realized that Jesus wouldn't move until she revealed herself, she bravely stepped forward.

> She came trembling; and failing down before him, she declared in the presence of all the people why she had touched him, and how she had been immediately healed. (Luke 8:47)

What Jesus asked her to do was unnerving. To publicly disclose her situation meant she deliberately got in contact with people. According to Jewish law, anyone who touched anyone unclean would also become unclean. In other words, she could not participate in family gatherings, celebrations, or religious activities. The fact that she suffered continuous bleeding meant she lived in isolation—a self-imposed exile. For her to enter the large group of people was bold. She could have easily incited the ire of people but she walked by faith and stepped out into the light. Jesus wanted her to come out from the shadows. She emerged and confessed to everything.

Then Jesus calls her, "daughter"—the only time Jesus uses this affectionate, familial term on someone. This was her spark point. Jesus took the extra step of healing her heart in addition to the physical ailment. He tells her she is beloved and not an outcast. Jesus didn't need to do this. After all, he was in a rush to Jairus's house to save his twelve-year-old daughter from "dying" (Luke 8:42) but Jesus had another "daughter" to save. He drew her out to ensure that her emotional wounds were also tended to. Jesus empowered her to publicly declare what God had done and helped her to find her voice again.

We haven't heard from her since this interaction, but we can imagine her rejoining her family and community. We already know about her strength as demonstrated by her determination to seek out Jesus amid the crowd. Now, her boldness will be exercised to express Jesus. People will no doubt wonder what happened to her after her long absence

Locate Spark Points

and physical ailments. With conviction, she will tell everyone it was Jesus.

Locate Spark Points

If you've never heard of religious "nones" as a religious marker, it is understandable. "Nones" had been a small minority but in the last ten, twenty years they have become a significant percentage of the US population.[101] In 1900, "nones" were for the most part nonexistent. "Nones" are those who describe themselves as religiously unaffiliated and they have, in 2024, risen to about 28 percent of US adults, according to Pew Research.[102] The largest of the "nones" are millennials and Gen Zers (those born between 1999 and 2015), the youngest generations (eligible to be surveyed) at 34 percent but baby boomers and Gen Xers are becoming more religiously unaffiliated. In 2007, 12 percent of boomers and 18 percent of Gen Xers described themselves as "nones"; in 2012, those numbers increased to 15 percent for Boomers and 21 percent for Gen Xers, a slight uptick but, statistically, according to Pew, revealed "significant margins" of increase.[103] The shift in American attitudes toward Christianity has been dramatic, especially when you compare that almost half of all Americans attended church from 1955 to 1958, which is "the highest percentage in US history."[104]

The rise of the "nones" indicates a much broader trend happening in America. People are turning away from religious beliefs and religious institutions. "With a few exceptions," according to Pew, "the unaffiliated say that are *not* looking for a religion that would be right for them. Overwhelmingly, they think that religious organizations are too concerned with money and power, too focused on rules and too involved in politics."[105] Interestingly, most "nones" say they were raised in Christianity. "Yet today," Pew research states, "they tend to be disconnected from religious institutions. Not only have they shaken off religious *labels*, they also have largely shaken off involvement in churches, synagogues, mosques and other religious organizations."[106]

By every measure, people's interest in church is declining and the situation will not get better according to data. While people are becoming less religious and don't affiliate with religious traditions, their interest in supernaturalism is spiking. In 2023, *National Geographic* reported that the number of Americans who identify as "pagans" has increased 100 percent since 2001.[107] At an evangelism conference, I asked the audience made up of pastors and active laypeople what people think and feel about church. Here are some of their answers:

- "Skeptical."
- "Suspicion."
- "Rejected. Not good enough. Toxic. Hurt."
- Judgmental. Abuse. Enabled toxic behaviors."
- "Growing interest in indigenous religions."
- "Division in the church."
- "Church has weaponized shame against them."

- "What's the point? It makes no difference."

People's responses certainly capture the negative perception weighing on the church but there was, however, a comment from the audience that I had never heard before: "Pagan reconstructionism. Thor."

At first, I wasn't sure if he was serious. I asked, "You mean, Thor, like in the comic books?"

"Exactly," was his reply. He is a millennial pastor and has seen many from his generation who grew up Christian turn to paganistic religions. I was skeptical. I asked him to tell me more about the Thor religion. He went on to describe the Thor rituals and principles and their belief system. I was stunned that such a religious phenomenon exists at all but it is an indication of the mounting unhappiness and frustration that finds expression in non-Christian directions.

Researchers tell us paganism in America, as a whole, is on the rise. Paganism, an umbrella term that includes occult, witchcraft, crystals, sorcery, and magic, has spread further on social media. An example of paganism on social media is "witchtok," for the witchcraft hashtag (#WitchTok) which has over eleven billion views on TikTok and over seven million posts on Instagram. Witchcraft, which has long been viewed with suspicion, something like a fringe activity in the margins of society, has "transmuted into a mainstream phenomenon."[108]

What we are witnessing is the increased decoupling of Christianity and churches in the lives of Americans. According to Barna, nearly two-thirds of people aged eighteen to twenty-nine who grew up going to church "have dropped out."[109] Among the reasons for why they dropped out, one-third said church is "boring" (31%). One-quarter thought "faith is not relevant to my career or interests" (24%) or that "the Bible is not taught clearly or often enough" (23%). "Sadly," Barna concluded, "one-fifth of these young adults who attended a church as a teenager said that 'God seems missing from my experience of church.'"[110]

What we see happening on the surface only tells part of the story. The evidence clearly shows people leaving the church. At the same time, however, people demonstrate interest and curiosity about spirituality. A major shift is happening as people don't view the church as a place that connects with them at a deeper level. Now more than ever, there is an urgent need for churches to reevaluate what constitutes effective evangelism.

Culture has significantly changed in the past fifty years, but churches remain rooted in their institutional outlook, a reality that creates blind spots. Many evangelism programs fall flat because of blind spots that prevent church leaders from seeing people as they are and understanding their urgent concerns. For example, consider the most pressing issue raised by Varun Soni in the previous chapter. How would churches respond to the question, "How do I make friends?"—a question that Soni gets from students. This is a question that he "never got" in his first five years as the Dean of Religious Life at USC.[111] Nowadays, he gets asked that question "almost daily from students." This is their spark point.

Speak to Spark Points

As Soni noted, this trend is not an isolated instance but a nationwide phenomenon. The demand for mental health services is increasing and colleges are having a hard time keeping up. The usage of counseling centers has "greatly outpaced" the increase in student enrollment.[112] In 2018, Cigna, one of the largest health insurance companies, surveyed twenty thousand adults and published the US Loneliness Index, revealing loneliness at epidemic levels.[113] The study showed that all age groups experience loneliness. Still Gen Z in particular experiences loneliness more acutely as they "fall to the bottom" among all generations in the loneliness index.[114]

The explanation of their situation is not a call for churches to become counseling centers but rather to shine light on a pressing concern that is profoundly felt by young people today. Weaving in the most compelling, urgent, and serious matters in the drafting of evangelism is crucial, because understanding what's really driving these outcomes helps to better target the particular spark points. When we speak to spark points, we shift the attention away from institutional goals, which may have little to do with what's deeply meaningful to the target audience, to the individual. When we do evangelism with the spark points in mind, we see the world through their eyes and relate Jesus in a way that makes sense to them.

CHAPTER SEVEN

Be You in Christ

Many years ago, I was the pastor of a church in the Poconos Mountains of Pennsylvania that first began a German-speaking congregation by the Pennsylvania Dutch in the nineteenth century. There, I was introduced to Pennsylvania Dutch culture and their unique foods, such as dandelion salad with hot bacon dressing, *fastnachts* (German doughnuts), and the wide assortment of pies.

Pork and sauerkraut dinner is one of the few cultural traditions that continue in the church. Usually served in early January, eating pork and sauerkraut in the new year was meaningful to the Pennsylvania Dutch as it symbolizes prosperity for the coming new year. Known as the national dish, sauerkraut, made from cabbage, a round vegetable shaped like a coin, is associated with good fortune.

However, most customs and traditions have slowly disappeared, but they have not been forgotten. The older members reminisce about the past when Pennsylvania Dutch cultural festivals and traditions were regularly on the church calendar, like the strawberry festivals, pie sales, and women's circle. The arrival of large discount stores made the work of women's circle obsolete but the older members will tell you that it was more than just making quilts.

When women's circle was an active part of the church, women came together on a weekly basis to quilt. At first, women came together out of necessity. A thick quilt or comforter can take six hundred to a thousand quilting hours, translating to a few months or up to year. Women coming together to quilt was a way to support one another in a very practical way but it was much more.

In a women's circle, six or ten women would sit in a circle with a quilting frame in the middle. Quilting is a communal activity requiring constant communication, teamwork, coordination, and artistic creativity. While quilting thick comforters takes the most effort, backpacks, stuffed hearts, dolls, pillow covers, quilted throws can be done at a quicker pace.

In Pennsylvania Dutch culture, a quilt symbolizes love. Hand-stitched quilts are given as a wedding present, bereavement gift, or baby shower present. Receivers of quilts know what it involves to make one, and knowing that loved ones stitched them makes it more special. Makers of the quilt know that their quilt will help a newlywed get through the cold winter months. Quilts are a family heirloom. It is not uncommon for families to possess quilts made three or four generations earlier. You can find quilts displayed like artwork hanging on the walls of Pennsylvania Dutch houses.

Quilting as a group requires patience, not just for the time and effort to make one but also for working with young girls who are just starting out. They pass down their knowledge to the next generation while the youngsters, working alongside elders, listen to their words of wisdom. From family to family, generation to generation, quilting passes down important cultural knowledge. Women strengthen emotional and spiritual bonds and expand their social network while quilting. They laugh, share stories, and concerns with one another.

When cultural activities combine with Jesus, an evangelistic and missional element is infused into the activity. The act of quilting itself is not an evangelistic activity but, when intertwined with Jesus, a Christian outlook is woven into the fabric of the activity. At the heart of the women's circle is "spiritual time." A long-time member said, "We always have a devotional and share our needs, our prayer concerns."[115] If a concern was shared during women's circle, they would stop what they were doing and pray for her and her family. If something more was needed, like funeral arrangements and reception, which the Pennsylvania Dutch community took very seriously, they would mobilize to meet the grieving family's needs.

At times, Christians participating in a cultural activity may transform it into a godly endeavor. "What's most important to remember is that we are doing this for the glory of God," a member said.[116] "In the early years," she says, "women made clothing for local needy people, flannel baby layettes (blanket, baby gown, diapers, and bibs) and they crocheted booties."

The need was great in their community and they managed to sew just about anything they could get their hands on. She added, "Women also took (livestock and chicken) feedbags and trimmed and hemmed them to become sheets and bolsters."[117]

As time passed, they made comforters and quilts for local people in need and for domestic and international missions. They donated quilts to Christian Aid Ministries and Northern Light Gospel Mission, which work with Indigenous populations. As you can imagine, shipping large and heavy comforters and quilts is costly, especially overseas. They offset the significant shipping costs by selling their quilts. The profit "all goes to the quilting-comforter project here at the church."[118] The money is also used to buy more material and supplies for comforters and quilts.

Some churches donated quilts to local hospitals and organizations. They would make flannel baby layettes (baby gowns, blankets, diapers, and bibs) for new moms. At another church, the women's circle honored a close member of the church family who died by collecting all his shirt ties and creating a quilt top. The spirit and memory of a loved one now continue to literally warm the heart as a quilt.

"Be you in Christ" means you and Jesus are enough. When we do what we love to do and infuse it with Jesus, we become authentic witnesses. "Be you in Christ" should not feel like work. The women's circle shows how simple everyday activities could be adopted for Christian witness. If we, for example, take inventory of our associations, we can see that we belong to many communities, subcultures, and groups. In every subculture, say, a bowling league, hiking club, or fans of a particular team, each has its unique traits and language. For example, if you belong to a hiking club, you have inside cultural insight to know the concerns and issues related to hikers. You would know what uniquely excites hikers and, conversely, what makes them particularly upset about hiking. You essentially are a cultural native to your subculture.

Old Bethel in New York's Pier 11

Facing the East River in New York's Lower Manhattan, Pier 11 is strategically located. Commuters from New Jersey, Upstate New York, and other boroughs regularly ride ferries to Pier 11, which is minutes by foot from Wall Street. Four subway lines are also within a short distance that take people across Manhattan. Commuters are not the only ones who use Pier 11. Local residents for example can catch a ferry to Brooklyn while enjoying a panoramic view of the city and the Statue of Liberty.

Although Pier 11 is known today mostly as a destination for commuters and visitors, it was in the nineteenth century a hub of the city's commerce and immigration. Shipping was the primary way business was conducted in the nineteenth century, and Manhattan's numerous waterfronts all around the island provided ample space. By 1840, more ships carried cargo and passengers entering New York's ports than all other harbors in the country combined. Fifty years later in 1890, New York became one of the busiest in the world.

Permanently moored at Pier 11 in 1845, "Old Bethel" was a condemned ship, meaning that it was no longer fit for service before the Methodists of New York bought the ship and repurposed it into a "floating church"—a ship-church on the waterfront. The remodeled ship came complete with a sanctuary with a pulpit and pews in the cargo space, quarter-deck cabin converted to a classroom and sexton's apartment, and a room in the bow renovated as the pastor's office.

How did they come up with buying and refurbishing an old ship and making it into a floating chapel? Pier 11 was a popular port for Scandinavian ships. Thousands of Scandinavian sailors sailed into New York every year but there was a small problem: They hardly ventured outside the port. There was a good reason for that. They were on standby. Once they entered the Pier, they assisted with the unloading and disembarking. They had a brief respite but it wasn't too long. Once the ship was cleared, new cargo and passengers filled the ship and they soon left New York.

The Methodists decided to bring the church to them on a familiar venue, a ship. Scandinavians are renowned as seafaring people and, while a floating church ship is certainly unconventional, it brought a sense of familiarity. They recruited Olof Hedstrom (1803–1877) for this unusual evangelism but he was ideal for the job. Hedstrom, a former Swedish sailor, converted to Methodism after he landed in New York and committed his life to preaching and ministry. He understood, better than most people, the harsh livelihood of Scandinavian seamen. He knew the physical and emotional toll their work exacted on them because he was one of them.

On May 25, 1845, in Pier 11, Hedstrom preached his first sermon in Old Bethel to more than fifty people.

If you were Scandinavian and your ships arrived at Pier 11, you could not help but notice Old Bethel. Old Bethel flew the Swedish flag, as well as American, Norwegian, and Danish flags. A huge sign draped over the side of Old Bethel declared that it was a "house of God."[119] Another sign on the ship invited people to come on board for conversation, reading materials, and Sunday worship. Hedstrom would "meet all incoming ships from Scandinavian countries" that entered Pier 11, visit those on board the ship, distribute Bibles, sermons, and tracts, and invite them to visit Old Bethel right there in Pier 11 for service, Swedish snacks, conversations, or reading materials.[120]

Few could have imagined that Old Bethel, a floating church in Pier 11, would leave an imprint on the development of Swedish American Christianity. Olof Hedstrom would bring his younger brother Jonas to the United States, and Jonas converted to Christianity and became a Methodist preacher. Jonas and his family migrated west and settled in northwestern Illinois where he became "the acknowledged founder of Swedish Methodism in the West."[121] Jonas Hedstrom worked as a blacksmith during the day at his shop but in his off hours he shared Jesus. "He preached in English in the schoolhouses about Victoria [a town Hedstrom co-founded], and also in Lafayette, Knoxville, and elsewhere."[122]

Hedstrom's evangelistic efforts were so successful that "conversions occurred at almost every service."[123] In one year alone, it was reported that "thirty thousand immigrants were served in some manner by the Bethel Ship and its staff."[124] The enthusiastic response to Jesus among Scandinavian immigrants resulted in many returning to Sweden in order to share Jesus with their hometowns. Largely due to converted lay Swedish immigrants who returned to Sweden and evangelized their kin, Sweden in 1900 "had the largest Methodist community on the [European] Continent" with over fifteen thousand adult members.[125]

At Pier 11, could an American have succeeded as well as Olof Hedstrom? Possibly but Hedstrom had many advantages. Not only did he speak the language, he knew their customs and traditions. He knew what touched their hearts and spoke of Jesus, which was related to their most pressing need from their cultural point of view. In many ways, Hedstrom was being himself. He was exactly in the same situation as they were. He came to America as an immigrant from Sweden. He worked in shipping. Then, he encountered Jesus in America, which ignited a holy combustion.

Soon Hyun—the Horseback Riding Korean Pastor

When Soon Hyun and his wife Maria Hyun left Korea and arrived in Hawaii in 1903, he never expected to do anything more with his life in Hawaii than work as a contract laborer on the Hawaiian plantations he signed up to work on. The sugar plantations had become a booming business in Hawaii, so much so that a 1906 US government report stated that "all industries" in Hawaii "are ultimately dependent upon the sugar industry."[126] Plantation owners recruited laborers from East Asia including Korea to work on the sprawling campuses that resembled the size of a large state university. These "camp towns," as they were called, were built throughout the Islands and the largest plantations housed more than twenty thousand people to plant, harvest, mill, boil, and refine sugar cane. Families lived on these plantations and Alice Hyun, Soon and Maria Hyun's first child, was born in 1905 on the Waipahu plantation.

While working on the plantations as a laborer, Hyun did not know at the time how he already possessed qualities for evangelism. In 1903, very few Koreans knew how to speak English but Hyun did. In Korea, he converted to Christianity and conversed regularly with American missionaries who taught him English. He became so proficient that missionaries hired him as a translator. Not only did Hyun know English but, after having spent so much time interacting with American missionaries, he was also familiar with Western culture, which was completely foreign to other Koreans on the plantation.

Little did he know when he first arrived but Hyun came to realize the unique qualities he possessed. In addition to his long workday, he began to teach English to fellow laborers in the evening. Hyun was soon recognized by fellow Koreans. They installed him as their unofficial leader. Hyun became so proficient at resolving issues between the plantation management and Korean laborers that the plantation hired him as a mediator and interpreter for the Koreans in the camp.

As a Christian, Hyun also helped organize a Korean church in the camp town. Because a church building was unavailable, they gathered at makeshift worship spaces. In other plantations, "boardinghouse kitchens" became a popular location for Korean worshippers to gather on Sundays.[127] Hyun's leadership and evangelism were recognized by the local Methodist church in Hawaii, which hired him as a preacher.

He did so well that the Methodist Church appointed him over the entire island of Kauai, the "Garden Island" as the pastor/preacher for the Korean community. "There, traveling on horseback, he covered the island from one end to the other, taking care of the sick, arranging schooling for the children, and conducting religious services."[128] His work was so impressive that plantation owners took notice and "began making regular financial contributions."[129] Through their support, Hyun built the first Korean church on Kauai, on a hill near Lihue.

Japanese Americans and Mochi

If you've never heard of mochi, they are soft dome-shaped, milky-white Japanese pastries made of chewy rice. They are served Japanese restaurants as mochi ice cream. They can be found at your local supermarket. Mochi is eaten all year round but it has special meaning for the New Year. Two mochi are set on New Year's Day, a small mochi atop a larger mochi that looks like a snowman. It represents the young generation, the small mochi, resting atop the older generation, the larger mochi, symbolizing the generational support and connection between them.

Making mochi from scratch is a labor-intensive process that requires a small army of people to work together, from steaming, grinding, molding, and pounding with wooden mallets. Making mochi all day will leave your head and hair covered in dusted cornstarch. Sherman Kishi of Livingston United Methodist Church in Livingston, California says, "It takes us from eight in the morning until at least two in the afternoon [to finish]."[130]

The Japanese Americans at Wesley United Methodist Church in San Jose, California, have been grinding and pounding mochi at their church for the past forty years for New Year's Day. The tradition wasn't started as a fundraiser or a special activity. They were just being themselves. After the sweet rice has been soaked overnight and later steamed, the doughy mass gets put into a large granite bowl where the pounding starts. A long wooden mallet is used to pound the dough relentlessly to smoothen it.

The tradition is an occasion for everyone in the community, across generations, to come together to work side by side. At a certain point, something interesting happened. Non-Japanese people from the neighborhood took notice and started appearing for the mochi-making festival. Not only did they show up, but they also began to volunteer. They got their hands on a long wooden mallet and started pounding the dough.

The mochi-making festival became a gateway for people to attend church, but it wasn't intentional, which may be the reason why it succeeded. They came precisely because Japanese Americans had no agenda other than being themselves. Japanese culture, especially food and pop culture, has become popular and, from a freestyle perspective, a spark point for people to become interested.

The same situation happened at a Korean church in North Carolina where my children attend. Over the years, non-Korean teens joined the youth group just because they followed K-pop, K-drama, and Korean food. They're studying the Korean language and immersing themselves in everything Korean. I guest preached there a few times and on one occasion I sat at a table with non-Koreans after service. I was curious how they found out about this church. One person said she, one day, came for the Korean church's annual food festival where they sell Korean food to the public. She said she enjoyed the experience so much that she decided to come for Sunday services.

Living Nativity

When Dr. Pati Graham, in the introduction, received the challenge to create your own evangelism project at the evangelism conference, she returned to her church in Bryson City, North Carolina, with enthusiasm and got to work. Christmas was coming up, and she wanted to go outside the church walls and tell her city about Jesus without being overbearing and preachy. She wanted her community to encounter Jesus in a fresh and engaging way.

In just two months, she produced and directed "Living Nativity," a live-action adaptation of the nativity scene. In total, sixty-five people were involved in the production, including sixteen actors. She and fellow organizers conducted a casting call for the sixteen roles that also included children. On the church's YouTube channel, you can watch videos of church members as well as locals auditioning for the roles of Herod, wise men, angels, Joseph, and others.

The crew members built the interactive outdoor nativity crèche in front of the church, which is on Main Street, the city's main thoroughfare. She got wardrobe that matched the clothing of ancient Judea. No, they didn't have a live baby, but "Living Nativity" was made to look as authentic as possible to a scene in ancient Bethlehem. They decided to launch the production a week before Christmas for two days in the evening when commuters walked by the church.

People in Bryson City were hit with Christmas in a way they did not expect. They were treated to a staged reenactment of the birth of Jesus. Actors in historical custome and appearance performed their roles in front of the carefully decorated set. A campfire next to the crèche was the site of children's story time: the retelling of the birth of Jesus. Children were invited over to roast marshmallows over the fire to make s'mores while listening to campfire stories. Passersby received a paper bag filled with an apple, an orange, candy, nuts, and something extra for the children.

"Living Nativity" could not have been possible without the unwavering support of Pastor Wayner Dickert who not only encouraged her from start to finish but also partook in the event. Freestyle's success in the local church relies on the church leaders to expand their definition of "evangelism" because freestylers will sometimes come up with ideas that have never been done before.

Many evangelism models operate from the "us-them" approach where the "doers" are evangelizing the "receivers." In the "us-them" model, people understand the objective of evangelism. The "doers" are the active participants while the "receivers" are the passive audience. Freestyle doesn't operate on a "us-them" paradigm. More like a "you and Jesus" approach, freestyle enables individuals to express Jesus in their own way.

Dr. Pati Graham felt like an "unbridled horse" while doing her evangelism. Unbridled horses are unleashed, untamed, bold, carefree, and free-roaming in the wild. Don't we all want to feel like that? For many Christians, evangelism is unwanted, something to avoid and run away from, but evangelism, done from a freestyle perspective, is how believers can feel alive.

Preparing for "Living Nativity" was infectious. The project created a "buzz" in the church and community. More people in church got on board and offered to help. In the preparation leading up to the event, she made sure non-church people and church members who had been neglected were in the cast. She invited an eighty-year-old from the church to be the king in "Living Nativity." He was thrilled. He shared that he had not been asked to do anything in the church and he loved the opportunity to participate. "Living Nativity" took place outdoors in the evening when it was colder. She was concerned that he might not come for the second night since it was forecasted to be even colder, but she was delighted to see him. He came with a cheerful attitude and said he wouldn't miss it.

She was thrilled to see church people and non-church members "working alongside" one another in a "retelling of Jesus." Residents appreciated how the church went "outside of church walls" to reach out to them. Passersby thought the church created goodwill by going out of the church and reaching out to people (especially in the cold weather). So many people walked past it and stayed and to watch. One local resident said he didn't know there was a church there. I later learned that the project was "an enormous amount" of work; it was hard trying to get everyone and everything together. Through it all, if you were to ask her if it was worth it, she would say yes. She said the entire production led to the "best turnout" in the community.

Because "Living Nativity" was a passion project, doing it did not feel like work. As it often happens with holy combustions, the fire spreads to other people or continues to burn, which was the case at Bryson City. The experience with "Living Nativity" was so rewarding and fulfilling that she decided to branch out into the Lenten season. She and Bryson City prepared and completed a live-action adaptation of the Last Supper the following year. In chapter 9, "There Are No

Failures," I discuss how a single combustion can cause additional fires as embers of the fire scatter to the surrounding areas.

Freestyle as Relief to Clergy

"Pastors are tired," says a bishop in the Evangelical Lutheran Church in America (ELCA). The impact of COVID lockdowns exacerbated the situation. Relationships with and among parishioners suffered during the lockdown, political divisions were increased, and fights over COVID protocols ensued. Jungling saw how pastors were "giving a lot of themselves to help folks deal with the trauma of the pandemic. They've had to face polarization in their own congregations, people's anger and frustration about masks and vaccines, whether to have worship or not."[131]

The pandemic destabilized clergy as they faced unprecedented disruptions to congregational life. Clergy had to weather through unprecedented challenges that upended central aspects of church life such as gathering, worshipping, and connecting. Clergy across the country endured what Barna called a "burnout epidemic." In a 2021 study, Barna "discovered that nearly four in 10 pastors had considered quitting full-time ministry in the past year, a number that rose even higher in 2022."[132] Recent research by Barna shows that clergy confidence had rebounded since pandemic lockdowns were lifted but remains below the pre-pandemic numbers.

While the pandemic has left many clergy disillusioned, it has also disrupted the church-going culture of people. When social distancing was enforced, churches were closed. Many churches streamed their services online in its wake but the stoppage had far-reaching consequences. When churches eventually reopened, many people didn't return, as much as a third of practicing Christians didn't return to church, according to Barna. "We're not going back to normal," said David Kinnaman, president of Barna Group. "I think we're going to see is a really interesting sort of 'new normal,' a lot of deep disruptions that are going to take place over many months and maybe even many years."[133]

The time apart from church worship and activities exposed hidden weaknesses in the church. "We have to retrain people from the beginning on why you should bother to assemble," said Collin Hansen, author of *Rediscover Church: Why the Body of Christ Is Essential.*[134] As people stayed home during the lockdown, they questioned their assumptions about their churchgoing ways. Hansen added, "I think pastors take that for granted and are going to be surprised how many people never had that vision to begin with and never come back when the all-clear is given." Kinnaman predicts "church leaders are going to revert to doing things the ways they've always known them" after the lockdowns are lifted and in-person services resume.[135] However, as Kinnaman warns, a fundamental shift has occurred whereby practicing Christians question the "role and relevance of the church." He adds, "The gap between the church and society is only going to be larger as we rebuild the church in a post-pandemic world."

Traditional evangelism is top-down where church leaders organize and lead evangelism projects, while the laity follows the ideas provided. Freestyle upends the traditional model by having the laity take the initiative. Freestyle mobilizes everyday Christians by empowering them to be themselves in Christ. In general, Christians do not believe they are equipped for evangelism. They don't believe that they have what it takes to engage in evangelism. In freestyle evangelism, they already possess all that they need: "Be You in Christ." No additional training or education is required. They have within themselves the resources to release Jesus to the world.

CHAPTER EIGHT

Freestyle Can Be Messy

In the 1970s, it became clear to Pastor A. Adrienne Howard that she and her church needed to do something about their situation. Her church faced what was an existential moment in its long history. She was the pastor of Albright United Methodist Church in the Bloomfield neighborhood in the heart of Pittsburgh's East End. For decades, Albright had seen a steady erosion of the population that once filled the church's pews. Howard wrote, "Urban seemed somewhat inadequate to describe the Albright United Methodist Church."[136] Albright, built in the Gothic Revival style of architecture that was common for Protestant churches in the early twentieth century, is "shadowed on all sides by fast food restaurants, small groceries, laundromats, real estate agencies, upholstery factories and high-rise apartments."[137]

Like many cities in the Northeast, Pittsburgh saw a wave of white flight to the suburbs that transformed the city's neighborhoods, including Bloomfield. But that wasn't all. For years, Howard wrote that her neighborhood "faced the problems common to city churches—suburban flight and urban blight, higher costs and lower incomes being only the

Freestyle Can Be Messy

obvious ones."[138] Recently, things have gotten a little better but problems remain as Howard states, "urban blight is still here, although suburban flight is lessening."

For a long time, Albright survived on a core group of members but they were shrinking in number every year. Anyone who knows Albright's situation can see how the downturn impacts the congregation. Howard said, "Energy levels are sapped and we pray that they will be renewed."[139] For the church to survive, the answer was all too clear: They needed to increase church attendance and membership. Howard said, "Albright had to make changes." The future of Albright was at stake. The obvious solution was evangelism.

Albright started to map out what they wanted to do and put aside resources to reach their goals. They employed denominational programs as well as other popular methods used by churches. Howard said they, for years, tried "*all* [emphasis mine] of the standard methods of self-resurrection and a large variety of church growth methods."[140] Albright's evangelism in fact went beyond what you would typically see churches do. They fanned out to "the streets where they live" to hand out flyers about their church and approached neighbors with invitations to join them for worship.

To welcome newcomers, they became more conscientious of hospitality. They greeted them when they came, talked to them during service, and encouraged them to come again. They redoubled their efforts at evangelism. They did everything known to them but "they did not work," Howard bluntly said. "Their traditional method of spreading the gospel was falling on deaf ears and hardened hearts."[141] Evangelism methods and practices that had been the mainstay of Christian outreach in the past were no longer effective in an ethnically diverse neighborhood with many divergent subcultures. Evangelism models that succeeded so brilliantly in the 1950s and 1960s had the effect of conforming people to a prescribed "church culture" that no longer interested people. Many at Albright became disheartened, frustrated, and disillusioned after years of engagement.

At this moment, Albright reached a critical point. After making serious attempts but failing to draw people, they could have easily given up—a decision that would have meant a slow but inevitable death. To their credit, Albright chose the less-traveled road, a bold decision that was fraught with risk. The unfamiliar path meant there were no maps, guides, or road signs to guide their way.

They wondered how they should proceed. Their Bloomfield neighborhood became ethnically diverse over the years. Today, if you drive over the Bloomfield Bridge and into Bloomfield, you are greeted by a large sign: "Pittsburgh's Little Italy." But it's not just Italian Americans. Asians, Hispanics, and African Americans all made Bloomfield their home and they brought their differences. The members at Albright realized outsiders cared little about Albright's church traditions, distinctive legacies, or the stalwarts of the churches they were supposed to revere and follow.

It's hard not to be affected by the decline of membership but Albright wasn't ready to abandon ship yet. They took the courageous step of venturing into the streets to engage their neighbors with a radical agenda: to have no agenda and simply get to know them. Howard said, "Going out and spending time in the neighborhood's variety of settlements provided the answer."[142]

By any measure, this was bold. In doing so, they chose to see the "other" for the first time. They saw neighbors as they really were, not as people to Christianize, but as ordinary people with the same everyday struggles and issues as everyone else. The people at Albright saw how brilliant and how unsettling and how unique they were. Howard said, "They are laughingly, frighteningly, blessedly, different."[143]

Howard: Don't Homogenize People

The people in the neighborhood were not—by any stretch of the imagination homogenous, but, yet, Howard realized, Albright's evangelism was, essentially, an attempt to homogenize them—to make them look, act, worship like them. Howard's insight led her to write an article, "Homogenizing Is Only for Milk."[144] Published in her denomination's church newspaper in 1980, Howard criticizes the institutional church not for its promotion of evangelism but for ignoring what its mindset and approach to evangelism actually do to people at the local scene.

Evangelism is the church's effort, according to Howard, to make people "church broke."[145] Howard reveals the church's underlying assumption of evangelism, of using evangelism as the means to break people into their respective church. Using evangelism as a way to assimilate people into church has been so normalized that we continue to repeat this practice. A consequence of "church broke" evangelism is that people have to fit in in order to be accepted. Howard discovered that, through her interaction with her neighbors in Bloomfield, they don't want to be broken in. People simply want to be themselves in church—not to take on the church identity of a dying congregation.

Nearly forty-five years after she penned the article, Howard's warning to the church continues to ring true. When we think about evangelism, we implicitly view our neighbors as the "other" that needs to become like "us," making a "us-them" division in our perception—as opposed to enabling them to be themselves and to express Jesus their way. In other words, evangelism is the instrument the church uses to make outsiders become like us. At Albright, realizing the "homogenizing" effect of evangelism was the first step toward reframing how they understood and practiced evangelism.

If not "homogenizing" the newcomers, what are the other options? How else could we relate to those outside of our church community? Howard said, "Celebrate the differences of course."[146] The approach, however, is not without its pitfalls—the same openness that welcomes differences also invites church members to think about themselves and their relation to outsiders. At Albright, issues quickly arose as they opened things up. For one, Albright's worship service was steeped in the mainline Protestant tradition, something that congregants strongly felt attached to. Howard described her congregation as "homogenous in values and life styles."

Freestyle Can Be Messy

The diverse neighbors of Bloomfield were hardly a match for Albright's homogenous church culture. Instead of trying to make them conform to their traditions, Albright created autonomous spaces for them. Albright opened their church to a Korean-speaking congregation that was looking to provide its own service. Albright also created a separate service for street children, families and friends devastated by alcoholism, and a community of deaf people. In essence, she enabled subcultures with their distinctive concerns to be themselves to encounter Jesus.

As Albright discovered, when these subcultures were enabled to freestyle, without any pretenses or agendas, it empowered them. It released them to self-initiate and freely minister to one another. "They come together in common need," Howard said. If you are, for example, an abandoned street child, you are likely to feel most comfortable with other street children who truly understand the unique issues that you have to endure on the streets. It would be difficult to imagine a street child, with his or her tattered clothes and shabby appearance, blending with those in their Sunday best on Sunday mornings. After all, who better than another street child to minister to the struggles of another street child? Howard observed, "They worship, educate, succeed, fail, cry and rejoice in their own tradition or lack of it."[147] In other words, Albright's new framework released members of different communities to share Jesus in ways that spoke to their particular locations in life.

Because the idea of "homogenization" serves as a powerful directive in how we understand evangelism, people may wonder what theories or models of evangelism the people at Albright are following. What is the goal of Albright's evangelism? What is their endgame? Howard says, "There is no goal."[148] In other words, releasing people to worship God is the point. If there is an objective, Howard says it is "all these [groups] find their own expression of faith."

Evangelism, in other words, isn't the effort to make everyone sing to the same tune but rather to support them in producing their own music according to their unique style. Under Howard's leadership, Albright began to practice evangelism in a different way but it didn't come without pushback and challenges. When you invite a cacophony of peoples under one roof, there are bound to be issues working together. Howard says, "We do not always understand each other. Sometimes it seems we rarely do." And, yet, the different ministries "bring us all together." Howard added, "The goal is to weave the fabric for which only the church of God has the thread."[149]

Making a Mess

Albright's experiment brought more than what they bargained for. Cultural differences and misunderstandings exacerbated the frictions between groups. Howard wrote,

> We suffer the sins of suspicion and distrust, of false pride and unspoken fears. We waste time and energy grieving for what once was and wishing for an easier way. While seeking understanding and praise for what we do, we hold our counsel closely, fearing

Freestyle Can Be Messy

condescension and competition. We pray for forgiveness and guidance.

Tensions underneath the surface continue to simmer, as some Albright members wonder if all the trouble is worth the aggravation.

"Success?" Howard asks, as if she anticipated the question of her peers who wonder if the results are worth all the strife. She answers, "The pews are not as full as they once were but there are no cobwebs. If the noise is often strife, it is more life than the sacred silence of ecclesiastical entombment."[150] "The sacred silence of ecclesiastical entombment" is Howard's way of describing the mindset of churches that prefer self-enclosure to the messiness that compelling evangelism produces.

Pastor Howard's experience is an excellent example of how churches can work with diverse peoples and subcultures without expecting them to lose themselves. The experiment worked because Albright empowered distinct communities to thrive on their own but such allowances didn't come without problems, as Albright had to contend with challenges on various fronts. Howard acknowledged that opening up their church space and hearts produced messy situations but she prefers the noise of people doing ministry to the alternative: the "silence of ecclesiastical entombment" that Albright was inevitably headed toward.

Introducing freestyle to congregations will bring messiness. Freestyle ministries and evangelism will not be tidy. Freestyle encourages a free-form style that releases respective groups to grow and develop on their own. Albright set terms and boundaries but unfamiliar styles and manners can test them.

Pastor Howard chose not to focus on the mess but rather on the people, a decision that enabled her and her congregation to see people in an authentic way. This is much harder than you might think. Many Christians can't get past the idea that a ministry in their own church produces a mess. Freestyle will cause a mess of varying degrees because it invites openness, spontaneity, and creativity. The element of risk is inherent in freestyle and that itself will repel some Christians. Institutional Christianity reveres orderliness and tidiness but freestyle enables freedom for people to explore new spirit-led directions.

Some Christians are so concerned about things going out of hand in church that they miss opportunities to spark combustions in their community. As we consider what Albright went through, let's not lose sight of how important Pastor Howard's bold pastoral leadership was in the constantly evolving, messy situation. Many churches resist change because it introduces unwanted disturbance to what they've always done. Freestyle invites new strokes, styles, and modes of evangelism. As freestylers find their way, they expand the frontiers of what we think of as evangelism, which might be unsettling.

"I Hate Free-Range Chickens!"

Elliott Homestead is set on a two-acre rolling farmland near the Columbia River in Washington. The place is what people think of when they imagine a picturesque rural landscape—except the minute you step into the homestead, free-range chickens are getting into everything. Before they decided to put up boundaries, these free-range chickens became a nuisance, so much so that Shaye Elliott, who runs the homestead with her husband and children, said, "I hate free-range chickens."[151]

Why not let the chickens free-range wherever they want? They did and learned the hard way about the mess that they leave behind. For one thing, she's on a never-ending egg hunt. Hens lay eggs everywhere and she means everywhere. She's found loose eggs in the shrubs, the house, the tomatoes, the neighbor's dog kennel, the haystack, buckets, the cow shelter, and anywhere else imaginable. They have no sense of "off-limits."

That includes poop. She finds chicken poop on toys, golf cart, children's shoes, grills, hay, firewood, the greeting mat, tables, coats, and so forth and so on. "No surface is sacred from their defecation," she says with a sense of resignation. On one Sunday morning, "we got in the car for church, only to realize that a car door had been left open." It was too late by the time she discovered that there was "a giant chicken poo smear on the back of my maxi dress."[152]

In addition, chickens are good eaters and they will eat almost anything. It is wonderful when they help eliminate spiders, ticks, ants, and other critters that run around the farm but, when they start eating your berries, lettuce, spinach, and other greens, there's a problem, but that's not all. They will also scratch and stomp on the veggies to shreds. Elliott learned her lessons from the experience and made safeguards to ensure they don't get into places where they shouldn't but, despite the mess they make, she remains a firm believer in free-ranging.

Doing freestyle evangelism will feel a little like what Shaye Elliott went through with her free-range chickens. You're not exactly sure where freestylers will go and the mess they may create in the room where they are given space to roam and explore. Freestylers, with their gifts and calling, are released to the world. They don't exactly fit into a mold. Many of them won't look like what we think evangelism should look like.

On the other hand, the way we do evangelism in the church is quite predictable. The roles and desired outcomes are clearly defined for church volunteers. That is not to say that they don't make a difference. Many find meaning and fulfillment, but flexibility is not part of the plan. If we continue the analogy of free-range chickens, the opposite of free-range is chickens raised in large factory farms where caged chickens have little room to maneuver. The objective in these places is for chickens to produce eggs, but not just any kind of eggs. They need to look the same. When you go to your local supermarket and inspect the eggs in the carton, they look exactly alike in shape and color.

However, free-range chickens produce eggs of a variety of colors and shapes. If you ever shop for eggs on a working farm and open an egg carton, you'll discover that no two eggs look alike. Some have the shape you'd expect, others do not. You may be surprised to find most eggs are bespeckled and ruddy-looking in different shades.

Freestyle Breaks the Mold

Think for a moment about how you would feel if you discovered a messy evangelism program at a church. Most of us, I think, would have a difficult time imagining any church ministry as messy since we expect them to be well managed, orderly, and problem-free; otherwise it may not be approved.

For churches, freestyling can be scary and unsettling, because it allows for people to explore and discover themselves in the act of expressing Jesus. Just as Shaye Elliott learned with her chickens, roaming chickens make a mess. If you enable freestylers, you are potentially inviting a messy situation. Not all freestylers, obviously, will make a mess but it is a distinct possibility.

In his ministry, Jesus habitually combusted people, an outcome that drove the Pharisees crazy. The Pharisees thrived on religious rules and regulations, to which they placed themselves in charge of enforcement. They prized order and structure and they let people know about it. When Jesus combusted people, the Pharisees were not too far behind criticizing the mess that Jesus had made.

Freestyle

In the Gospels, the Pharisees closely followed and watched Jesus's every move. On one occasion, they watched Jesus to see whether or not he would violate the Sabbath by curing a man with a withered hand. Jesus made a mess for them when he cured the man's hand and the Pharisees "were filled with fury and discussed with one another what they might do to Jesus" (Luke 6:11). They didn't like it when Jesus associated himself with people they disapproved of. They "grumbled" and said in disbelief, "This fellow welcomes sinners and eats with them" (Luke 15:2). They were watching Jesus again and saw that his disciples were plucking heads of grain to eat while walking through a cornfield. They came to Jesus and said, "Look, your disciples are doing what is not lawful to do on the Sabbath" (Matthew 12:2). The Pharisees would no doubt drive out the freestylers from their midst.

Freestyle Expands Boundaries

On September 16, 2008, New Yorkers witnessed a strange sight on its bustling streets: chickens literally crossing a road. Chickens and a turkey stood on the corner of Second Avenue and 125th Street as if they were waiting for the walk signal to change.[153] As to how these chickens "free-ranged" themselves onto the streets of Manhattan is a mystery. Witnesses say they roamed around a vacant lot near a gas station but migrated to the street corner. A passerby at a nearby bus station quickly got her phone out to take photos. She said, "I have to send my friends pictures or else they would never believe we have chickens on 125th Street."[154]

Freestyle Can Be Messy

New Yorkers pointed out that the chickens are trying to scratch a living in the big city just like everyone else. A bystander said, "We're all struggling through these hard times, and the chickens are struggling to survive, too." He continued, "They find freedom on the city streets, and once they find freedom, they can eat and survive."[155] Sympathetic drivers honked at the chickens to warn them of the incoming traffic. A construction worker across the street saw them run out on the road. A few of them didn't make it. He said, "I've already seen two of them get run over. It's a shame, because they're cool chickens."[156] People were relieved when New York City's Animal Care and Control Center was called to the scene and recovered the remaining runaways.

The chickens were misfits on the streets of Manhattan and free-ranging will sometimes take us to unforeseen places. Freestyle attracts misfits because they are allowed room to figure out their abilities, talents, and calling in Christ. Does your church allow for misfits? Or are they frowned upon until they conform? Misfits are like Zacchaeus and the Samaritan woman who don't look the type to religious authorities.

We can only imagine their reaction when Zacchaeus and the Samaritan woman began their evangelistic campaign. Things get messy quickly. Jesus uncorked their enthusiasm and everyone around them was shocked at their response to Jesus. Freestylers will test and unsettle boundaries and challenge many of our notions.

Pastor Adrienne Howard witnessed the mess that her evangelism caused when Albright boldly decided to enable nontraditional groups to flourish. The mess at Albright caused division within her congregation. Howard acknowledged the costs of her decisions. She said, "Energy levels are sapped and we pray that they will be renewed. Old members have left in hurt and anger, and they are missed. Whether we will survive is a question rarely asked anymore, although it still lingers in the shadows beneath the surface of any venture."[157] I've encountered churches—even as the prospect of extinction was staring right at them—resist any measure that may unsettle how they did things. They would rather go down with the ship than loosen their grip on the steering wheel. While many church members left in frustration, Howard understood this was the price of the evangelism that they started. She added, "Evangelism? Yes, we know we live by grace, but we are here and our neighbors are beginning to hear the good news."

CHAPTER NINE

There Are No Failures

In the fall, squirrels are busy collecting acorns. If you see them grabbing and shaking an acorn, there is a good reason. Researchers discovered that squirrels can detect how healthy an acorn is by shaking it. If the acorn rattles, they can tell that the acorn is damaged in some way. Perhaps an insect has eaten into it. Squirrels will eat the damaged ones.

What do they do with the healthy ones? People think squirrels store acorns in trees but it's too risky. Squirrels are notorious thieves and they will steal each other's acorns if given the opportunity. What do they do? They bury them in the ground where other squirrels can't see them. But with so many squirrels around and watching, there is the chance that they may steal their acorn. If they sense that another squirrel is watching, they will pretend to bury the nut, then later bury it in a different place when no one is looking. Sometimes squirrels have "acorn anxiety"—the fear that their acorn will be stolen. They've been known to dig up acorns and take them somewhere else to bury.

When squirrels find a suitable place, they dig a tiny hole, approximately an inch below the surface, and deposit them, but they don't put acorns in one hole. That too would be risky. They bury individual acorns all over the place, ensuring they have food for the coming winter.

With so many acorns everywhere, how do squirrels ever find their hidden stash of nuts? First, researchers have discovered that squirrels have extraordinary spatial memory about where they've buried the nuts. They've shown the uncanny ability of locating them over a wide distance. In addition, they can detect the scent of nuts in the soil. The scent of the nut and particular soil is so unique that they can detect it even through a layer of snow.

And squirrels bury a lot of acorns—a lot more than what they would need. Perhaps they are accounting for lost or stolen acorns. Researchers estimate that squirrels recover only 10 percent of their buried acorns. That means nine out of ten acorns stay buried in the ground. What is interesting about this situation is that squirrels greatly contribute to the planting of oak trees. What's more, by burying acorns far and wide, squirrels ensure the success of oak seedlings since the parent tree won't shade them out. Now, let's think on a grander scale. Consider that one squirrel in the fall months can bury as many as one hundred acorns a day. That is a lot of future oak trees they are sowing in the ground. It is estimated that oak trees in North America were populated in a significant way through the work of squirrels.

Squirrels are a good example of what freestylers are doing. The mission of freestyle evangelism is scattering seeds. In the life of an acorn that becomes a full-grown oak tree, a squirrel's role is small but critical. In freestyle evangelism, we say "there is no failure" because it doesn't operate by a success-failure paradigm. Freestyle is not measured by a specified outcome of what it should look like in the end. The point of freestyle is to simply scatter seeds and invite God to do the rest. In Mark 4:26–29, Jesus said,

> The kingdom of God is as if someone would scatter seed on the ground, and would sleep and rise night and day, and the seed would sprout and grow, he does not know how. The earth produces of itself, first the stalk, then the head, then the full grain in the head. But when the grain is ripe, at once he goes in with his sickle, because the harvest has come.

Unfortunately, evangelism in churches can become so tethered to numerical goals that Christians may be setting themselves up for failure. In the church, evangelistic goals are often linked to quantifiable data. How many new members have joined? How many come for Sunday worship? By what percentage has the church grown over the past year? How many children attend Vacation Bible School from year to year? When we evaluate evangelism based on data, Christians will no doubt feel a sense of failure and disappointment, especially when you consider the unabated overall decline of Christianity in America over the past sixty years.

In freestyle evangelism, failure and success are not points of reference used as benchmarks to measure evangelism because individuals' faith journeys are a work in progress. For example, let's say a seed is sown in a person's heart twenty years ago but has remained mostly dormant. For whatever reason, they walked away from the gospel and lived as if God didn't matter. After considerable time, however, another encounter with Jesus ignites the seed, causing it to germinate and grow fruit.

When people experience holy combustions, expect to be surprised by what comes next. In Mark 4:30–32, Jesus said,

> With what can we compare the kingdom of God, or what parable will we use for it? It is like a mustard seed, which, when sown upon the ground, is the smallest of all the seeds on earth; yet when it is sown it grows up and becomes the greatest of all shrubs, and puts forth large branches, so that the birds of the air can make nests in its shade.

Jesus warns us not to assume anything just because it doesn't look right. A tiny spark can impact the entire church or neighborhood or city. Jesus illustrated this point using yeast flakes as an analogy. "The kingdom of heaven is," Jesus says, "like yeast that a woman took and mixed in with three measures of flour until all of it was leavened" (Matthew 13:33).

Freestyle shifts our attention from success as the mission of evangelism to the faith journey itself. Freestyle takes an expansive, holistic, and long-term view of evangelism. From our human perspective, an evangelism project may look like a failure, but the newly sown seed may need time to break through the hard soil or lie dormant underneath the surface, waiting for the next person to water it. There's an element of mystery to the whole process that freestyle takes into account. In the end, God causes holy combustions, even in the most unlikely of places.

Freestylers Scatter Seeds

The primary task of freestyle is to scatter seed and expect God to take over. The seed scatterer in the Parable of the Sower distributed seeds indiscriminately or, in other words, all over the place. When we hear the word *broadcast*, we usually think of TV radio waves that are sent as over-the-air signals but the word has agrarian roots, specifically as the act of sowing seeds. The word is a combination of *broad* and *cast*: *broad* meaning wide, open, and extended and *cast*, an act of tossing, throwing, or hurling something with your hand. When television networks adopted the word broadcast, they described the transmitted audio and video content sent over the airwaves intended to reach the widest audience.

Ecclesiastes 11:1 says, "Cast thy bread upon the waters; for thou shalt find it after many days" (KJV). The verse gives an unusual instruction: to toss bread upon the waters. The very act of throwing bread upon the waters seems counterintuitive, a waste of good bread. Some scholars believe the "bread" references seed since bread is made from milled seeds of grain. Why would anyone toss something valuable onto the water? Seems risky and unnecessary. Why not cast seed or bread on healthy soil instead? The verse acknowledges the difficulty of people casting their bread upon the waters, and the second part of the verse states, "For thou shalt find it after many days."

Certainly, casting one's bread upon the waters seems pointless and wasteful but the Bible urges us to take the risk and act on faith. Venture out into the unknown. You never know what a good return you may receive. When we cast bread out into the waters, we don't know if we will ever get it back. If we think it will return, we have no idea when. To cast bread is a leap of faith as it requires a measure of confidence in God that we shall find it again.

"Casting thy bread" is an act of trust. We are not completely sure how but we trust God that we shall indeed find it again. The Bible explains the necessity of faith overcoming our doubts and fears later in the chapter:

> You do not know the work of God, who makes everything. In the morning sow your seed, and at evening do not let your hands be idle; for you do not know which will prosper, this or that, or whether both alike will be good (Ecclesiastes 11:5–6).

Jesus Sends Out Sowers

In the Parable of the Sower, the sower broadcasts seed everywhere, landing on paths, rocky spots, soil with many thorns, and good soil. As you can imagine, seeds that fell on the path did not fare very well as they couldn't penetrate through the hard surface. Birds came and ate the seeds on the path. Some may say throwing seeds on the path was a waste. Why throw away good seed to the path? It is a valid point, but that is not the way this sower works.

When Jesus sent out his disciples for an evangelism mission (Matthew 10:1–14, Mark 6: 7–13, Luke 9:1–6), the objective was to broadcast gospel seeds far and wide. They were instructed to subject themselves to the mercy and kindness of the people they encountered. To ensure that the disciples were utterly dependent on the hospitality of locals, Jesus told them to "take no gold, or silver, or copper in your belts, no bag for your money, or two tunics, or sandals, or a staff" (Matthew 10:9–10). Jesus knew that not everyone would welcome the good news. If they encountered anyone who didn't "welcome you or listen to your words (v. 14)," Jesus told them to just move on: "Shake off the dust from your feet as you leave that house or town" (v. 14). By humbling his disciples and making them completely reliant on the goodwill of local people, Jesus made sure that his disciples shared the gospel from a lower position, as opposed to a higher (and, possibly, condescending) position.

One benefit of evangelism from a lower position is that we are less likely to judge or condemn. The lower position also ensures that we engage people with a grateful heart. We would listen more closely to them, instead of talking at them or doing evangelism to them. Even when it seems like they've rejected the gospel, we don't know how the seed may germinate later. People's soils are constantly changing with the passage of time. Life happens and the different ebbs and flows of life affect our receptivity to the gospel.

According to the season of people's lives, the gospel's impact will vary. Jesus broadcasted gospel seeds wherever he went but didn't find "success" everywhere. At times, he met stiff resistance, such as the time when he returned to his hometown of Nazareth. They were "astounded" by Jesus. They could not fathom how Jesus could do all these things. They muttered among themselves, "Where did this man get all this? What is this wisdom that has been given to him? What deeds of power are being done by his hands!" (Mark 6:2). Then they remembered Jesus's parents and siblings. Their understanding of Jesus as a person from their neighborhood prevented them from seeing Jesus as the Messiah. "And they took offence at him" (v. 3). How they dismissed his teachings, his "wisdom" and his "power" surprised Jesus as he "was amazed at their unbelief" (v. 6).

The possibility of God working in any kind of soil is central to freestyle evangelism. Zacchaeus the chief tax collector, by any measure, was a tough soil. Tax collectors were seen and treated as lowlifes and Jesus was mocked for associating with them. "Look [referring to Jesus], a glutton and a drunkard, a friend of tax-collectors and sinners!" (Matthew 11:19). Tax collectors were thieves, oppressors, and traitors to Jews and Zacchaeus was the chief of them. The fact that Zacchaeus was "rich" (Matthew 19:2) rankled many in Jericho, a high-profile city in ancient Judea, where many Levites and priests lived.

While Zacchaeus was wealthy, we can only imagine his emotional state. Being treated like a pariah in society could not have been easy. Every time he walked out into the city streets he could see the look of disgust in people's eyes. They sneered as he walked past them. We do not know Zacchaeus's exact tipping point. Perhaps it was when Jesus looked right into Zacchaeus's soul and saw his inner pain and yearning for acceptance.

His combustion was a powerful moment. We can imagine tears running down from Zacchaeus's face as he felt, perhaps for the first time, true acceptance from God. The joy was irrepressible. Zacchaeus couldn't help but release his excitement. Although the NRSV translates his statement in the future tense, Zacchaeus is speaking in the present tense in the original Greek, which is why other versions say, "See, Lord, I am [now] giving half of my possessions to the poor" (Amplified), and "Here and now I give half of my possessions to the poor" (NIV). As the Amplified version and NIV indicate, Zacchaeus could have started handing out money at that exact moment—in the presence of Jesus and the crowds, including priests and Levites, that gathered around them.

Can you imagine the scene? Zacchaeus telling his servants to bring out his treasury and distributing money right away? And to watch people squeal with delight as money was handed to them? It must have been a wild spectacle. To the skeptics, they witnessed a surreal scene: The worst man in town is transformed before their eyes. What a glorious mess!

The transformation was real. He gave money away and promised to pay back double to anyone he cheated. Watching the circus-like atmosphere unfold, Jesus says to the crowds, "Today salvation has come to this house, because he too is a son of Abraham. For the Son of Man came to seek out and to save the lost" (Luke 19:9–10). If a Jericho resident or any stranger asks Zacchaeus, "What's happened to you? You are so different now!"

Zacchaeus's answer is always the same: "Jesus."

Don't Worry About "Success"

Another reason why freestyle evangelism doesn't operate on a success-failure paradigm is that, in the grand scheme of things, we may be working in a segment or part of a much larger journey. If you think about your spiritual journey, important figures who've had a transformational influence in your life will invariably come to mind. If we probe deeper, however, we can probably recall minor figures who've made a small but significant difference in our Christian walk, such as a casual conversation that stirred something warm within us or strangers who made us rethink something about ourselves or an off-the-cuff remark that pinged and stimulated our souls toward Jesus.

Chapter 18 in the book of Acts describes how Paul founded the church in Corinth, an important Greek city that is about fifty-one miles west of Athens. At Corinth, Paul "would argue in the synagogue" proclaiming "to the Jews that the Messiah was Jesus" (Acts 18:4,5). When they "opposed and reviled him" (v. 6), Paul "shook the dust from his clothes" and said, "From now on I will go to the Gentiles" (v. 6). In time, Paul started the first Christian church in Corinth and a community of believers began to emerge. In fact, Paul "stayed there for a year and six months, teaching the word of God among them" (v. 11).

After Paul left Corinth, Apollos later arrived in the city. Apollos "was an eloquent man, well-versed in the scriptures" (Acts 18:24). The Bible describes Apollos as a charismatic speaker who "spoke with burning enthusiasm" and fearlessly challenged anyone as "he powerfully refuted the Jews in public" (v. 25, 28). Apollos was critical in building up the nascent Corinthian church, so much so that rival camps emerged: One side followed Paul and the other Apollos (see 1 Corinthians 3). Paul strongly disapproved of the division within the Corinthian church, but he had no issue with Apollos. Paul saw him as a "co-laborer" of the gospel. "For we are God's servants," Paul says, "working together" (1 Corinthians 3:9). In Titus 3:13, Paul instructs Titus to tend to Apollos's needs: "Make every effort to send Zenas the lawyer and Apollos on their way, and see that they lack nothing."

Paul calls out the Corinthian Christians for acting like "infants in Christ," "not ready," and "of the flesh" (1 Corinthians 3:1–3). Paul then corrects them on how they should view him and Apollos. In verse 6, Paul says, "I planted, Apollos watered, but God gave the growth." Paul obviously played a crucial part as the founder of the church. Apollos later arrived to develop the church further but each person had a part that was suited for the season of the Corinthian church. But, in the end, "God gave the growth" and God is the one who ultimately enabled the people's hearts and minds to turn to Christ.

From a freestyle perspective, evangelism is an opportunity for Christians to have a role in the larger design for what God has in store for individuals and groups. Some of us are planters, others waterers. There's no telling when, where, or how the growth will come. We trust that the bread will return one day but that is not our preoccupation. This understanding of evangelism is like the layering principle that Paul described. "Like a skilled master builder," Paul says, "I laid a foundation and someone else is building on it" (1 Corinthians 3:10). Paul here expresses a long-term view of evangelism. While he planted this church, he certainly won't be the last. While others will come and add to what he started, he reminds the Corinthians that servants bring their own unique set of gifts and skills. "Each builder must choose with care how to build on it" (v. 10). Paul says each builder is responsible for what they do:

> Now if anyone builds on the foundation with gold, silver, precious stones, wood, hay, straw—the work of each builder will become visible, for the Day will disclose it, because it will be revealed with fire, and the fire will test what sort of work each has done. (v. 13)

Paul calls Jesus the ultimate foundation. "For no one can lay any foundation other than the one that has been laid; that foundation is Jesus Christ" (v. 11). Christ is the foundation and generations of faithful believers have been adding layers and layers even before we came onto the scene.

Becoming Comfortable with the "Unknown"

People's receptivity to the gospel is constantly evolving—never static, since people go through different things at different times. Before the soil becomes fertile and ready to hear the gospel, the soil may need to be loosened up. The "turning over the earth" principle considers the preliminary (and thankless) work of loosening up hard surfaces, like the path in the Parable of the Sower, that aerates the soil for more circulation.

Take for example the Blue Christmas service that was mentioned in chapter 6. Pastor Nancy Walton took the bold step of including people from the neighborhood and enabling them to be themselves without pressuring them to conform. The results were powerful. God worked in the moment and everyone there knew they were a part of something special. An unexpected warm, accepting, and affirming spirit emerged from the service. It was as if a pressure valve released the tension built up over time.

There were no declarations of faith or conversions that resulted from the service but everyone knew something happened. We have a role in continuing and expanding the spiritual momentum as it happens. After the Blue Christmas service, a new window of opportunity opened that had not been there before. Who knows how long that window of goodwill and trust will be open? The window can close swiftly if old tensions and unresolved differences crop up. How can we continue the momentum by building confidence among the parties involved, including the stakeholders, to take bolder steps toward the unknown?

Step Out in Faith

"You give them something to eat," was Jesus's instruction to his disciples (Mark 6:37). You can picture their jaws dropping in astonishment. They could not believe what Jesus said. His instruction was a response to the disciples' plea to send the thousands of people away. They were in a remote area, people were hungry, and it was getting late. "This is a deserted place," his disciples said, "and the hour is now very late" (Mark 6:35).

Jesus could tell the disciples were very concerned about the lack of food. The situation looked dire. Jesus's reply was, basically: You do it. You figure out a way to feed them. The disciples were stunned. There were more than five thousand people. They retorted, "Are we to go and buy two hundred denarii worth of bread, and give it to them to eat?" (Mark 6:37). This is a polite way of saying, "You're kidding, right? Are you being serious, Jesus?"

Scholars say two hundred denarii equates to about seven months' wages. A massive amount of money, which they didn't have. Jesus knew this but he said it anyway to challenge them to think outside the box and to step out in faith. Some may say Jesus was setting up his disciples for failure since there was no possible way for them to get two hundred denarii, or at least that may have been what his disciples concluded. But Jesus wanted them to imagine the possibility with God, however impossible it may seem.

A similar incident happened on the seas. Have you ever gone boating at night in complete darkness? It was the middle of the night on the seas when the disciples saw a humanlike figure hovering on the water and it was coming toward them. "It's a ghost!" grown men squealed in terror. Jesus quickly pacified them, "Take heart, it is I; do not be afraid" (Matthew 14:26). Peter was scared too but something told him to seize the opportunity. He spontaneously yells, "Lord, if it is you, command me to come to you on the water" (v. 28). This was a crazy idea. The disciples were terrified when they saw Jesus. Now they turn to Peter and stare at him in disbelief as if he had lost his mind.

Jesus grants his request and says, "Come." Peter gets up and climbs over the edge of the boat and, miraculously, he stands on water. He doesn't understand how it's possible but he can feel the seas supporting his weight. He gleefully smiles, carefully takes his first steps, and starts walking toward Jesus. Things were going great until he notices the waves splashing against his feet and strong winds blowing on him. Then intrusive thoughts entered his mind, making him fearful. His doubts erode the faith that powered his miraculous walk; his body starts to sink into the water. "Lord, save me!" Peter cries out to Jesus. Jesus grabs and saves Peter and says, "You of little faith, why did you doubt?" (v. 31).

On the one hand, some may say' this was a failure. From a freestyle perspective, it was a great learning moment of self-discovery. Perhaps Jesus was even impressed that Peter managed to get a few steps in before he started sinking. If Jesus had never invited Peter to come out of the boat, Peter would have never known where faith could take him. If someone came up with a far-fetched idea in church, how likely would it be implemented? People may say it's too risky or they don't do that in this church. In other words, it's too messy for us to consider.

Who knows how Peter's experience may play out later? Peter embarrassed himself by sinking into the water but he and the disciples discovered an insight that they would not have received if Peter had not stepped out. Peter knows he can with faith walk on water (albeit only a few steps). Consider the disciples in the boat who witnessed an incredible, supernatural scene. The disciples were in awe after Jesus saved Peter and got into the boat. They said, "Truly you are the Son of God" (Matthew 14:33).

Conclusion

Have you heard of "dandelion parachutes"? It's a children's game played in a park or anywhere outdoors where dandelions are found. Children hunt the area for the best dandelion that they can find, which usually means a dandelion with the biggest crown—those tiny white globes of exposed seed also known as puffballs, parachutes, or, by its technical name, pappus. After everyone has one, children line up. On the count of three, they inhale as much air as possible and blow their hardest, releasing all the seeds into the air. They cheer on their parachutes to go and the one that goes the farthest wins.

The parachutes don't go too far when there is little or no wind. They float in the air for a while little and land a few feet away. However, if the parachutes catch a strong wind, they can really go. Did you know that a dandelion can travel as far as five hundred miles under the right wind conditions?

Over the course of *Freestyle* we've looked at a number of stories and illustrations like this—from moon soil experiments at NASA to the fire at Sumo Sushi restaurant in Madison to free-range chickens in a homestead in Washington—and what they all have in common is the element of surprise. When kids line up, ready to blow on their dandelion, they know everyone has a chance. No one has an edge to make their dandelion go farther than anyone else. It doesn't matter if you are the tallest, smartest, or strongest kid. The smallest child can win because the outcome depends on something outside of them, the wind. No matter how hard a child tries, success doesn't depend on effort. A big part of the fun is the surprise from watching the wind picking up drifting seeds and carrying them in unexpected ways.

This is the first lesson of freestyle. Practicing freestyle evangelism requires reliance and trust in the fresh wind of the Holy Spirit. Interestingly, the word for wind in Hebrew is *ruach*, which translates to breath, wind, or spirit. *Ruach* can also refer to the Spirit of God. The earliest usage of the word is in Genesis 1:2 where *Ruach Elohim*, or the Spirit of God, hovers over the waters. "The spirit of God" (*Ruach Elohim*) came upon Zechariah in 2 Chronicles 24:20. In one of the most famous psalms, David in Psalm 51:10–11 uses *ruach* twice with two meanings:

> Create in me a clean heart, O God, and put a new and right spirit (*ruach*) within me. Do not cast me away from your presence, and do not take your holy spirit (*Ruach Ha-Kodesh*) from me.

The theory of freestyle requires that we reframe how we think about evangelism—from a human-based enterprise to a Holy Spirit-driven initiative. From the way many Christians commonly think of evangelism, it is a product mainly of human effort. We think of an evangelism initiative as an idea that conforms to our thinking about evangelism. When we regard the undertaking of evangelism primarily as the work of human hands, it is easy to exclude the Holy Spirit from the activity.

Traditionally, our approach to evangelism isn't always about evangelism but a multitude of priorities sometimes far removed from whom it is meant to serve. For one, the dissonance can result in an ambiguity on the part of believers about the mission of evangelism. Christians have an instinctive disdain for this kind of evangelism because there is something in us that feels disingenuous about the way it represents Jesus. Their resistance is not confined to a particular kind of evangelism but extends to the entire work of evangelism. Compounding the situation are feelings of guilt that arise from the religious pressure to do something that seems disconnected to their values.

Freestyle evangelism is unconventional because it does not fit within the framework of the evangelism projects people are busy constructing. The fact that freestyle thrives in ambiguity will no doubt unsettle many. Conventional evangelism relies on concepts and methods and freestyle offers none. In freestyle, the ideas for evangelism come from individuals or the everyday Christians in the pews. The individual's passion powers the evangelism forward. Upon hearing the call of the Lord, they take the initiative to get out of the boat and to step out into the unknown.

In many cases, freestylers will go against the grain of the church's established sensibilities to which everyone is supposed to follow. To the stakeholders in the church, freestyle represents a threat to how they've been doing things for a long time. However, if you look at it differently, freestyle initiatives are exciting adventures into the unknown.

The Older Brother as a Stakeholder

Think for a moment about the older brother in the famous Parable of the Prodigal Son (Luke 15:11–32) working hard in the fields. Wiping sweat from his brow, he toils under the hot sun. Without complaint, he's been going out and doing his job in the fields but one day he hears loud music and dancing in the distance. He tries to get a better read on where it's coming from. He walks toward his house and realizes the noise of a raucous party and smell of barbeque are coming from his home.

At this point, he is at a complete loss. He quickly scans his mental calendar and wonders if he perhaps forgot something. He can't think of anything so he calls over a servant to find out. A servant said, "Your brother has come, and your father has killed the fatted calf, because he has got him back safe and sound" (Luke 15:27). When he discovers what is going on, his demeanor turns to disbelief and fury.

He can't believe this is happening. The more he hears about his father's actions, the angrier he gets. His father dressed his younger brother in the best robes, put an expensive ring on his finger, and gave him sandals for his feet.

Then his father orders that *the* fattened calf be slaughtered and barbequed for the party. In the Near East, the fattened calf was separated from the herd and given extra care and nourishment to prepare for a very special occasion, such as a wedding. In the parable, the father kills the fattened calf for the younger son and tells everyone it's party time.

The older brother is so mad that he refuses to enter the house. He can't understand why his father would do this. At the very least, the younger brother should be groveling back for mercy. Instead, his father throws him a huge welcome home party. The younger brother has been a total disaster, mocking his family's good name. He squandered his inheritance on "dissolute living" and only returned after losing everything.

Servants rush to the older brother in the fields, trying to persuade him to come to the house and celebrate, but he refuses. He continues to fume and his outrage grows. The father hears how upset he is. He leaves the celebration and looks for him. He pivots from being a joyful host of the party to a somber, compassionate father who must now placate his furious son. He gently coaxes him to come home to welcome his little brother, which makes him even more mad. He lashes out at his father:

> Listen! For all these years I have been working like a slave for you, and I have never disobeyed your command; yet you have never given me even a young goat so that I might celebrate with my friends. (Luke 15:29)

You can hear the pain in his voice. He feels betrayed. He strongly disagrees with what his father is doing and isn't sure if he really knows his father.

The father's response shows how he and his older son saw the situation differently. The father says, "Son, you are always with me, and all that is mine is yours" (v. 31). The older son sees himself as a dutiful son and caretaker of the property. His self-understanding revolves around work or, more specifically, how well he does his work. The father's perspective could not be more different. The father wonders why his son thinks he's like a slave when he's the co-owner? Even so, the son is not dissuaded from what his father says and continues to vent.

From the older son's point of view, as long as he dutifully serves his father, he feels justified. However, for his younger brother who never took work seriously, he was the antithesis of his beliefs, which is why he couldn't understand or relate to his father. However, the father keeps trying to change his way of thinking about the situation, "This brother of yours was dead and has come to life; he was lost and has been found" (v.32).

From the perspective of many congregations, the older brother might look like the perfect church member. He is committed and loyal, a respected member of the church family who is devoted to the welfare of his church. He is a long-standing member who rarely misses a Sunday. He teaches Sunday school. He tithes. He's active on multiple church boards and committees. He does everything that is asked of him without complaint.

However, freestyle pushes us to think and act like the father. The younger brother obviously made a huge mess of his life but the father chose to focus on his redemption rather than on the mess he left behind. On the other hand, the older brother, like many people in churches, cannot stand messes, especially in people. The older brother prizes orderliness, proper execution of roles, and expects productivity. The younger brother has none of those things.

The older brother is exceedingly able at his job. The father's house, with the older brother at the helm, is, without a doubt, better run. He manages the affairs of the house with efficiency and effectiveness but, when you think about how far off his heart is from his father's, we may wonder who the real "lost" son is in the parable. In the end, the younger brother was *inside* his father's house celebrating; the older brother was *outside* the house watching the celebration.

Freestyle seeks to reframe evangelism away from its focus on house or institutional objectives to individual harvest in Christ. That is not to say that institutional goals are sidelined. In fact, freestyle increases institutional vitality. As we've seen in earlier chapters, freestyle evangelism projects garnered attention and interest from the local congregation and the larger community. Freestyle projects were a catalyst that led to more ideas and the most important distinction about them is that they developed organically in the grassroots.

All too often, our evangelism feels like work or something outside of ourselves. The uniqueness of the individual is often not included. On the other hand, freestyle relies, as a fundamental principle, on the individual's uniqueness to express Jesus. Because freestyle starts with the individual and his or her background and experiences, freestyle is designed to work in any community, subculture, or location. This was evident at the follow-up meeting where we heard about freestyle working in urban and rural settings, among young and older clergy, and in conservative and liberal neighborhoods.

We can only imagine the younger brother's response after witnessing his father's lavish reception. At that moment, all of his past wrongful assumptions about his father collapsed and an irrepressible sense of gratitude emerged from its wake. We don't know what the younger brother did after this transformative moment but we can be sure that he will be living for his father and, perhaps, working to help soften his older brother's crusty heart.

The moment could not have happened if the father had not quickly pivoted. When he returned home, the father changed everyone's schedule on the spot. He stopped whatever they were doing and told them to get ready to party. Freestyle requires bold flexibility to adapt quickly when moments arise. When the older brother pleaded with his father about why he did this, the father simply said, "We had to celebrate and rejoice" (v. 32). He could not wait. The moment was now.

Conclusion

Freestyle as Release

People shouldn't feel like they are *doing* evangelism while freestyling because they are simply being who they are. They are released in Christ to be themselves. To those who feel they have little or nothing to offer, remember the moon rock soil or beach soil. No one thought anything would grow from those soils but life happened. Think about the ninety-five-year-old Ruth Spence or twelve-year-old Isaiah Jarvis who've made a big difference by simply doing what they love to do. If we think of evangelism as following the Holy Spirit's initiative, the weight of the burden around evangelism disappears.

Freestyle is a grassroots movement. Everyday Christians are called to create their evangelism. In the process, the feeling of release is also felt by clergy who carry the burden of evangelism. I asked the audience at an evangelism conference what some of the implications of a declining church were. What do they see happening with their congregations as the situation worsens? Someone said, "Doom and gloom"; another, "Concern about legacy." Other comments relayed the sense of despair felt by many Christians in the church but a few comments stood out: "lovingly critique things" and "more pressure on clergy to do something."

As church membership and attendance decline, people turn to clergy for leadership. They expect their pastors and ministers to lead the church's evangelism. Freestylers would inject new life into congregations and, under the freestyle model, the role of clergy and church leadership is reframed as identifiers of potential combustions, discerners of the feasibility of freestyle projects, and cheerleaders of people's attempts.

Give God the Credit

Think about the evangelism of Zacchaeus and the Samaritan woman. Their response to Jesus was expressed with excitement and joy, without a hint of an agenda, which made their passionate appeal all the more authentic. The peculiar thing is that if someone had asked Zacchaeus or the Samaritan woman while they were praising Jesus what a tremendous work of evangelism they were doing, they would probably have looked confused and ask, "Who, me? I'm not doing evangelism. I'm just happy I met Jesus."

When freestylers express Jesus, they are being themselves and that kind of authentic expression is contagious. The authenticity infected people who participated in the stirring Blue Christmas service or the Bee Party. Holy combustions leave behind a trail of goodwill that breaks down barriers and the situation is ripe for more combustions to ignite but that doesn't happen by design or by human effort. The Holy Spirit is the one doing the heavy lifting to bring new life to tired souls.

The Lord brought Ezekiel to a valley full of dry bones in a powerful vision. The Lord instructed Ezekiel to prophesy to the bones. When he did, "suddenly there was a noise, a rattling, and the bones came together, bone to its bone" (Ezekiel 37:7). Then Ezekiel saw that sinews, tissues, and ligaments started growing on the bones and every organ appeared and skin covered them "but there was no breath (*ruach*) in them" (v. 8). They remained lifeless.

Then the Lord said to Ezekiel, "Prophesy to the breath (*ruach*), prophesy, mortal, and say to the breath (*ruach*), 'Thus says the Lord God: Come from the four winds, O breath (*ruach*), and breathe (*ruach*) upon these slain, that they may live'" (v. 9). Ezekiel obeyed the Lord and "breath (*ruach*) came into them, and they lived, and stood on their feet, a vast multitude" (v. 10). Here we have a scene of lifeless bodies strewn across the valley. While Ezekiel played an important role, the Lord God breathed life into them. Freestyle locates the power to the wind of the Holy Spirit.

However, the Holy Spirit chooses where to go and freestyle makes no presumption about the Holy Spirit's direction. As Jesus says, "The wind blows where it chooses, and you hear the sound of it, but you do not know where it comes from or where it goes. So it is with everyone who is born of the Spirit" (John 3:8). What we can do is be like children playing "dandelion parachutes" and give the initial breath that launches them. The dandelion parachutes are in the air and we have no idea where they're headed. We send them out and let the wind do the rest. Similarly, we release gospel seeds far and wide into the air and invite the Holy Spirit to carry them to a new home.

Acknowledgments

I am greatly indebted to Jae Lee, the district superintendent of the Smoky Mountain District of the Western North Carolina Conference, for supporting my vision and inviting me to speak at the evangelism conference in October 2022. Previously, I mainly spoke about my work to academic audiences but the positive responses from the conference and the follow-up meeting encouraged me to write *Freestyle* for the broader public. I am grateful to the participants who took time to test the model with their congregations and share their stories. Their valuable feedback helped me see important insights from their perspective.

Thanks to my students at High Point University for the stimulating conversations over the years about Christianity and culture, generational challenges, and the state of the church. I am grateful to my friends in the Department of Religion and Philosophy for their continuous support throughout the process.

The author owes gratitude to too many of his friends and colleagues to attempt here separate acknowledgment of all,

Acknowledgements

but much appreciation is due to Gayle Chandler and David Chun for reviewing the whole manuscript and for their valuable criticism and corrections. Special thanks are due to anonymous readers for their close reading of the manuscript, which has had an invaluable influence on its development. Needless to say, the responsibility for any and all errors or shortcomings in this book is mine alone.

Finally, my family provided endless support along the way, and I am especially grateful to my wife, Julia, and children, Elli, Elgin, Ella, and Ellen, for putting up with me while I was in my writing cave. *Soli Deo Gloria.*

Notes

[1] "Almost Half of Practicing Christian Millennials Say Evangelism is Wrong," *Barna* (February 5, 2019), www.barna.com/research/millennials-oppose-evangelism/.

[2] Ibid.

[3] Ibid.

[4] Ibid.

[5] Ibid.

[6] Ibid.

[7] Allison Barron, "'Evangelism': A Dirty Word?" *Boundless* (November 17, 2017), www.boundless.org/blog/evangelism-a-dirty-word/.

[8] Ibid.

[9] Bryan Stone, *Evangelism After Christendom* (Grand Rapids, MI: Brazos Press, 2007), 10.

[10] Doug Powe, "Evangelism: A Witness to Love Not a Dirty Word," *Church Leadership* (April 26, 2022), www.churchleadership.com/leading-ideas/evangelism-a-witness-to-love-not-a-dirty-word/.

[11] Ibid.

[12] Beau Crosetto, "Evangelism: Today's Christian Curse Word," *Campus Ministry Today* (June 16, 2021), https://campusministry.org/article/evangelism-todays-christian-curse-word.

[13] Ibid.

[14] Ibid.

[15] Allison Barron, "'Evangelism': A Dirty Word?"

[16] Ray Comfort, "Why I Avoid Using a Dirty Biblical Word," *Christian Post* (December 13, 2018), www.christianpost.com/voices/why-i-avoid-using-a-dirty-biblical-word.html.

Notes

[17] Debie Thomas, "Reclaiming the *E* Word," *Christian Century* 140:2 (February 2023), 34–35.

[18] Ibid.

[19] Allison Barron, "'Evangelism': A Dirty Word?"

[20] Leah Hidde-Gregory, "Evangelism: I Am Not Sure That Means What You Think It Means," *Central Texas Conference United Methodist Church*, www.ctcumc.org/evangelism-is-not-what-you-think.

[21] "We Asked 1,600+ Christians Why They Don't Share Their Faith," *Jesus Film Project* (July 23, 2020), www.jesusfilm.org/blog/christian-evangelism-statistics/.

[22] Ibid.

[23] Allison Barron, "'Evangelism': A Dirty Word?"

[24] Bryan Stone, *Evangelism After Christendom*, 10.

[25] Quoted in Clare Ansberry, "Why Middle-Aged Americans Aren't Going Back to Church," *The Wall Street Journal* (August 1, 2023), www.wsj.com/articles/church-attendance-religion-generation-x-6ee5f11d?mod=hp_featst_pos3.

[26] Debie Thomas, "Reclaiming the *E* Word."

[27] K. Kale Yu, *Understanding Korean Christianity* (Eugene, OR: Pickwick, 2019), 191.

[28] "Restaurant Building Fires," *Topical Fire Report Series* (Federal Emergency Management Agency, FEMA) 12:1 (April 2011), 1.

[29] Ella Torres, "Spontaneous Combustion of Tempura Flakes Blamed for Sushi Restaurant Fires," *ABC News* (July 16, 2019), https://abcnews.go.com/Health/spontaneous-combustion-tempura-flakes-blamed-sushi-restaurant-fires/story?id=64364119.

[30] In dry regions of the Middle East, a well was guarded and contested. "Abraham complained to Abimelech about a well of water that Abimelech's servants had seized" (Genesis 21:25).

[31] "The See You at the Pole Story," *See You at the Pole*, https://syatp.com/pages/press.

[32] Mary Alford, "Students Gather for See You at the Pole," *Arkansas Baptist News* (October 2, 2023), https://arkansasbaptist.org/post/students-gather-for-see-you-at-the-pole/.

[33] Ibid.

[34] Ibid.

[35] Kate Synder, "95-Year-Old Norwich Woman Makes Quilts for Soldiers," *Times Recorder* (November 10, 2014), www.zanesvilletimesrecorder.com/story/news/local/2014/11/09/year-old-norwich-woman-makes-quilts-soldiers/18771545/.

[36] For more information about the Foundation, see their website: www.qovf.org.

[37] Kate Synder, "95-Year-Old Norwich Woman Makes Quilts for Soldiers."

[38] Ibid.

[39] Charley Lerrigo, "Everywhere, Everywhere Christians Today," *United Methodist Relay* 25:3 (April 1980), 8.

[40] Ibid.

[41] Nancy Jang, "A Personal Witness," *United Methodist Relay* 22:6 (July-August 1977), 6.

[42] Ibid.

[43] Ibid.

[44] Ibid.

[45] Ibid.

[46] Quoted in Orlando Crespo, *Being Latino in Christ* (Downers Grove, IL: InterVarsity Press, 2003), 82.

[47] Ibid., 84.

[48] Ibid., 82.

[49] Ibid., 83.

[50] Ibid., 82.

[51] Ibid., 82–83.

[52] Nancy Jang, "A Personal Witness."

[53] Ibid.

[54] Ibid.

[55] Tommy McArdle, "Little Leaguer Comforts Pitcher Who Hit Him in Head with Ball," *People* (August 10, 2022), https://people.com/sports/little-leaguer-comforts-pitcher-who-hit-him-in-head-with-ball-just-throw-strikes-and-take-deep-breaths/.

[56] Elizabeth Merrill, "Sportsmanship, Friendship One Year After Little League Hug," *ESPN* (August 15, 2023),

Notes

www.espn.com/mlb/story/_/id/38157556/little-league-world-series-hug-viral-moment-sportsmanship-batter-hit-head-pitch.

57 Tommy McArdle, "Little Leaguer Comforts Pitcher Who Hit Him in Head with Ball."

58 Dakin Andone, "Little League Batter Hit in Head Embraces Pitcher in Inspiring Display of Sportsmanship," *CNN* (August 10, 2022), https://edition.cnn.com/2022/08/10/us/little-league-hug-batter-pitcher/index.html.

59 "[ESPN] How An Incredible Act of Sportsmanship Led to a Moment of Inspiration & Unlikely Friendship," *YouTube* (August 12, 2023), www.youtube.com/watch?v=7HmSSET1bCU.

60 Bryce Newberry, "Players Who Captured World During Viral Hug Moment Reunited at Little League World Series," *KPRC2 Houston* (August 23, 2022), www.click2houston.com/news/local/2022/08/23/players-who-captured-world-during-viral-hug-moment-reunited-at-little-league-world-series/.

61 "[ESPN] How An Incredible Act of Sportsmanship Led to a Moment of Inspiration & Unlikely Friendship."

62 Ibid.

63 "Oklahoma Little Leaguer Invited to First Pitch of World Series in Pennsylvania," *News On 6 KOTV* (August 23, 2022), www.youtube.com/watch?v=pLhyMFXS1TI.

64 Bryce Newberry, "Players Who Captured World During Viral Hug Moment Reunited at Little League World Series."

65 Ibid.

66 Ibid.

67 Bill Keeter, "Scientists Grow Plants in Lunar Soil," *NASA* (May 12, 2022), www.nasa.gov/humans-in-space/scientists-grow-plants-in-lunar-soil/. Also see Anna-Lisa Paul, Stephen Elardo, and Robert Ferl, "Plants Grown in Apollo Lunar Regolith Present Stress-Associated Transcriptomes That Inform Prospects for Lunar Exploration," *Communications Biology* 5:1 (2022), 1–9.

68 Ibid.

69 Ibid.

70 Ibid.

[71] Mallary Caudill, "A Young Farmer Thrives on Unusual Soil," *Corteva*, August 8, 2021, www.corteva.us/Resources/Stories-of-the-Land/farmer-thrives-unusual-soil.html.

[72] Quoted in Sue V. Hook, *The Dust Bowl* (Edina, MN: ABDO Publishing), 101.

[73] Gamaliel was renowned in his time as a "master" of Jewish Oral Law. In addition, he was *nasi* (president) of Sanhedrin, the supreme Jewish court.

[74] Avi Bajpai, "Oh My Gourd, This Pumpkin Sets a New NC State Fair Record. Here's How Much It Weighs," *The News and Observer* (October 14, 2021), www.newsobserver.com/news/local/article255003782.html.

[75] Matt Casada, "Chris Rodebaugh Is Setting Out to Grow the Largest Produce in West Virginia," *59 News*, September 13, 2023, www.wvnstv.com/news/chris-rodebaugh-is-setting-out-to-grow-the-largest-produce-in-west-virginia/.

[76] Amanda Larch, "Life Is Gourd," *Greenbrier Valley Quarterly*, October 31, 2022, www.gvquarterly.com/blog/2022/10/31/life-is-gourd.

[77] Ibid.

[78] K. Kale Yu, "Revisiting Lamin Sanneh's 'Western Guilt Complex' from a Grassroots Perspective," *International Bulletin of Mission Research* 46:3 (2022), 399.

[79] Aaron Zitner, "Americans Pull Back from Values that Once Defined U.S.," *The Wall Street Journal*, March 27, 2023, www.wsj.com/articles/americans-pull-back-from-values-that-once-defined-u-s-wsj-norc-poll-finds-df8534cd?mod=hp_lead_pos10.

[80] Ibid.

[81] Ibid.

[82] Clare Ansberry, "The Surprising Surge of Faith Among Young People," *Wall Street Journal*, April 24, 2023, www.wsj.com/articles/the-surprising-surge-of-faith-among-young-people-424220bd?cx_testId=3&cx_testVariant=cx_166&cx_artPos=5&mod=WTRN#cxrecs_s.

[83] Ibid.

[84] Ibid.

[85] Ibid.

[86] Ibid.

Notes

[87] Varun Soni, "There's a Loneliness Crisis on College Campuses," *The Los Angeles Times* (July 14, 2019), www.latimes.com/opinion/op-ed/la-oe-soni-campus-student-loneliness-20190714-story.html.

[88] Joe Gibson, "How I Managed Deep Existential Anxiety," *Medium* (September 29, 2023), https://medium.com/change-your-mind/how-i-managed-deep-existential-anxiety-5b1da751da4b.

[89] Ibid.

[90] "2023 Annual Report," *Center for Collegiate Mental Health, Penn State University* (2023), 2.

[91] Ibid.

[92] The survey "found that 44% of students reported symptoms of depression, 37% reported anxiety disorders and 15% reported having seriously considered suicide in the past year." Justin Heinze, "College Students' Anxiety, Depression Higher Than Ever, But So Are the Efforts to Receive Care," *University of Michigan Public Health News Center* (May 9, 2023), https://sph.umich.edu/news/2023posts/college-students-anxiety-depression-higher-than-ever-but-so-are-efforts-to-receive-care.html.

[93] "Denzel Washington on Why 'Fences' Needed a Black Director: 'It's Not Color, It's Culture'," *SiriusXM* (December 20, 2016), www.siriusxm.com/blog/denzel-washington-on-why-fences-needed-a-black-director-its-not-color-its-culture. For the video interview, see www.youtube.com/watch?v=9Ayf8Iny9Eg.

[94] Ibid.

[95] "2022 Annual Report," *Center for Collegiate Mental Health, Penn State University*, 5.

[96] Ibid.

[97] "Addressing the Unprecedented Behaviorial-Health Challenges Facing Generation Z," *McKinsey* (January 14, 2022), www.mckinsey.com/industries/healthcare/our-insights/addressing-the-unprecedented-behavioral-health-challenges-facing-generation-z#/.

[98] Jerry Riendeau, "FOBO: Gen Z's FOMO," *The Gospel Coalition* (January 8, 2023), www.thegospelcoalition.org/article/fobo-genz-fomo/.

[99] Ibid.

[100] *Mishnah Nedarim* 3:4. For a further explanation of the treatment of tax collectors in *Nedarim 3:4*, see www.judaism-and-rome.org/mishnah-nedarim-34.

[101] "The number of religiously unaffiliated adults remained below 10% from the 1970s through the early 1990s." "Nones" is a category for those who say they are atheist, agnostic, or "nothing in particular" in research and surveys. "Religious 'Nones' in America: Who They Are and What They Believe," *Pew Research* (January 24, 2024), www.pewresearch.org/religion/2024/01/24/religious-nones-in-america-who-they-are-and-what-they-believe/.

[102] Ibid.

[103] Ibid.

[104] "On a typical Sunday morning in the period from 1955-58, almost half of all Americans were attending church—the highest percentage in U.S. history." Jim Dueck, *Then, Now, and Why Now: Sixty Years of Change in Education* (Lanham, MD: Rowman & Littlefield), 75.

[105] "'Nones' on the Rise," *Pew Research* (October 9, 2012), www.pewresearch.org/religion/2012/10/09/nones-on-the-rise/.

[106] "Religious 'Nones' in America: Who They Are and What They Believe," *Pew Research.*

[107] Christine MacIntyre, "Paganism Is on the Rise—Here's Where to Discover Its Traditions," *National Geographic* (March 22, 2023), www.nationalgeographic.com/travel/article/where-to-go-to-explore-pagan-culture.

[108] Bianca Bosker, "Why Witchcraft Is on the Rise," *The Atlantic* (March 2020), www.theatlantic.com/magazine/archive/2020/03/witchcraft-juliet-diaz/605518/.

[109] "Six Reasons Young Christians Leave Church," *Barna* (September 27, 2011), www.barna.com/research/six-reasons-young-christians-leave-church/.

[110] Ibid.

[111] Varun Soni, "There's a Loneliness Crisis on College Campuses."

[112] Ibid.

[113] "Cigna U.S. Loneliness Index," *Cigna* (May 1, 2018), www.multivu.com/players/English/8294451-cigna-us-loneliness-survey/docs/IndexReport_1524069371598-173525450.pdf.

[114] Ibid.

Notes

[115] Brice Stump, "Church's Sewing Circle Stitches Threads of Love," *CBS News* (April 22, 2012), www.cbsnews.com/baltimore/news/churchs-sewing-circle-stitches-threads-of-love/.

[116] Ibid.

[117] Ibid.

[118] Ibid.

[119] Henry C. Whyman, *The Hedstroms and the Bethel Ship Saga: Methodist Influence on Swedish* (Carbondale, IL: Southern Illinois Univ. Press, 1992), 59.

[120] "Olof Gustaf Hedstrom (1803–77)," *General Board of Global Ministries of the United Methodist Church*, www.umc.org/en/content/hedstrom-olof-gustaf-1803–77. "Olof Gustaf Hedstrom was born in the province of Kronberg, Sweden. At age twenty-two, he shipped as a sailor on a vessel bound for South America. It was diverted from its course and in 1825, it entered the port of New York where it was sold. On June 11, 1829, he married Caroline Pickney and in the same year, under his wife's influence, he was converted and immediately became active in Christian work." Ibid.

[121] Ernst Olson, *The Swedish Element in Illinois* (Chicago: Swedish-American Biographical Association, 1917), 17.

[122] Ibid.

[123] Andrew Hansen, "Norwegian and Danish Methodism in the Eastern States," *Journal and Year Book with Historical Section of the Sixty-Forth Annual Session of the Norwegian-Danish Conference of the Methodist Church* (May 27–30, 1943), 62–63.

[124] Henry C. Whyman, *The Hedstroms and the Bethel Ship Saga: Methodist Influence on Swedish* (Carbondale, IL: Southern Illinois Univ. Press, 1992), 59.

[125] Charles Yrigoyen and Susan Warrick, eds, *Historical Dictionary of Methodism* (Lanham, MD: Scarecrow Press, 2005), 112–113.

[126] In 1906, the US Department of Commerce and Labor reported: "Directly or indirectly all industries in the Territory of Hawaii are ultimately dependent upon the sugar industry—the social, the economic, and the political structure of the islands are built upon a foundation of sugar." "Dominance of the Sugar Industry," *Bulletin of the Bureau of Labor* 13:66 (September 1906), 367.

[127] K. Kale Yu, "Hawaiian Connectionalism: Methodist Missionaries, Hawaii Mission, and Korean Ethnic Churches," *Methodist History* 50:1 (October 2011), 11.

[128] Peter Hyun, *Man Sei! The Making of a Korean American* (Honolulu: University of Hawaii Press, 1986), 27.

[129] Ibid. "Among them [plantation owners], the Wilcoxes and the Isenbergs became not only staunch supporters but also lifetime friends."

[130] Natalie Winters, "Local Church Keeps Japanese Tradition Alive," *Turlock Journal*, December 18, 2015, https://www.turlockjournal.com/news/local/local-church-keeps-japanese-tradition-alive/.

[131] Ian Lovett, "Houses of Worship Face Clergy Shortage as Many Resign During Pandemic," *The Wall Street Journal*, February 21, 2023, www.wsj.com/articles/houses-of-worship-face-clergy-shortage-as-many-resign-during-pandemic-11645452000?mod=article_inline.

[132] "New Data Shows Hopeful Increases in Pastors' Confidence & Satisfaction," *Barna* (March 6, 2024), www.barna.com/research/hopeful-increases-pastors/. "We saw a steep drop in the number of pastors who said they felt energized by their jobs and a large spike in the data indicating many pastors discouraged, depleted and defeated by their day-to-day work."

[133] Brandon Showalter, "One Third of Practicing Christians Not Watching Online Church Services During COVID-19 Lockdown: Barna," *The Christian Post* (July 12, 2020), www.christianpost.com/news/one-third-of-practicing-christians-not-watching-online-church-services-during-covid-19-lockdown-barna.html.

[134] Kate Shellnutt, "Why Church Can't Be the Same After the Pandemic," *Christianity Today* (July/August 2021), www.christianitytoday.com/2021/06/church-after-covid-pandemic-trauma-tension-healing-together/.

[135] Ibid.

[136] A. Adrienne Howard, "Homogenizing Is Only for Milk," *United Methodist Relay* 25:3 (April 1980), 5–6.

[137] Ibid.

[138] Ibid.

[139] Ibid.

[140] Ibid.

[141] Ibid.
[142] Ibid.
[143] Ibid.
[144] Ibid.
[145] Ibid.
[146] Ibid.
[147] Ibid.
[148] Ibid.
[149] Ibid.
[150] Ibid.
[151] Shaye Elliott, "Building a Chicken Run (and Why I Hate Free Range Chickens)," *The Elliott Homestead* (April 20, 2015), https://theelliotthomestead.com/2015/04/building-a-chicken-run/.
[152] Ibid.
[153] Corey Kilgannon, "Pecking, But No Order, on Streets of East Harlem," *The New York Times*, September 16, 2008, www.nytimes.com/2008/09/16/nyregion/16chickens.html.
[154] Ibid.
[155] Ibid.
[156] Ibid.
[157] A. Adrienne Howard, "Homogenizing Is Only for Milk."

Made in the USA
Columbia, SC
26 March 2025

f39977a1-fdf8-4af7-b489-8486e231f32bR01